Social Theory and Social Invention

Social Theory and Social Invention

Edited with an Introduction by
Herman D. Stein

Essays by Charles Frankel
Michael Harrington
Melvin Tumin
Gunnar Myrdal

Cleveland
The Press of Case Western Reserve University
1968

Introduction

Herman D. Stein
Dean, School of Applied Social Sciences,
Case Western Reserve University *

The extraordinary flow of inventions and technological development in recent decades, following upon advances in theory in the biological and physical sciences, is there for all to see. This connection between scientific theory and invention was not always so direct. It was only near the turn of the present century that the relationship became close.[1] Technology then began to follow science, with the time gap between the two becoming rapidly reduced. Theoretical work in genetics became the basis for experimentation on new strains of plants and animals with dramatic results for agriculture, the germ theory led to the development of new drugs, and the discovery of the electron opened up the vast field of electronics. The momentum of translation from science to technical invention has accelerated, with new technology pouring out of industrial, governmental, and university laboratories.

What is the relationship between social science theory and social invention? It is by no means as clear as in the natural sciences. There have been remarkable social inventions—in political organization, educational patterns, economic planning, legal and judicial systems, and welfare organization. Yet it would be difficult to extract from these developments very much that derives essentially from social theory and scientific investigation rather than from life experience, informed judgment, and political process.

Among the aspects of the science-technology relationship in the natural and physical sciences to which Henrik Bode refers are three which may have a bearing in the social field.

---

* Now Provost of Social and Behavioral Sciences, Case Western Reserve University.

[1] Henrik W. Bode, "Reflections on the Relation Between Science and Technology," in *Basic Research and National Goals* (March, 1965), National Academy of Sciences, Washington, D.C.

First, "the more complex disciplines necessarily lag behind the simple ones." Physics moved first because it is "simpler than chemistry"; chemistry, in turn, is simpler than biology, and biology is simpler than the behavioral sciences. "More and more areas are becoming accessible to scientific investigation, but the more complex areas have to wait longer than those that are simpler." The term "simpler" apparently refers to a greater measure of determinism and predictability.

Second, certain fields require the massive employment of techniques and tools as well as concepts from other scientific fields. Astronomy, for example, is completely dependent on other fields for its tools, particularly on physics, and high energy physics uses tools furnished by electrical engineering.

Third, "the application of science to technology does not happen by itself; it has to be brought about through some agency." It was not until the early twentieth century that the industrial laboratories began to make technological use of scientific discoveries. In the science-based industries, enormous effort is required to develop the necessary technologies for the proper utilization of science. "A good example is furnished by the development of the transistor. The transistor itself arose from a deliberate and aggressive effort to exploit the new field of solid state physics. To support the work, however, one needed competence in a variety of related areas. Crystallography was one, for example...." [2]

The first two considerations are well recognized as they pertain to the social sciences. In the sense in which Bode uses the term, the behavioral and social sciences are indeed "complex" disciplines. Not all key problems lend themselves to scientific investigation, particularly where essential variables cannot be controlled or where undesirable manipulation of people would be required for proper experimental conditions. Moreover, the level of predictability, while higher than commonly assumed, is of a much lower order in the social than in the physical field, since the range of possible interactions, unforeseen conditions, and non-controllable variables in the former is far broader. Even demographic projections, where the variables can be specified with increasing precision, are subject to considerable error, let alone predictions of crowd behavior or family

[2] Bode, "Reflections," p. 68.

disruption or types and nature of deviant behavior, or the consequences of given measures of social control.

The utilization of tools as well as concepts from one field in another as a prelude to major advances is also well understood in the social sciences as being necessary but not yet fulfilled. While efforts at cross-disciplinary approaches are increasing, it is as yet most difficult to pull together useful tools and concepts from diverse fields, such as economics, sociology, political science, psychology, and anthropology for attacks on fundamental problems that cut through all of these disciplines.

It is the third of the aspects referred to, the context within which the application of social theory to social invention can most productively and fruitfully occur, that should receive the most urgent attention. We do not as yet have the equivalent of the industrial laboratory through which to test and exploit social theory in order to develop technology in the interests of society. It may be noted parenthetically that the industrial and commercial fields make incidental use of social science, in limited ways related to their own requirements. Advertising agencies, for example, make use of mass communication and stratification theory as well as motivation theory; and adaptation of theory and technique related to organizational behavior is also utilized. Major social inventions have not, however, flowed from such use.

Where does one look for substantive investment in the translation of social theory into application? The federal government does subsidize social research and increasingly is concerned about its utilization, but the investments are minor compared to those in the biological and physical sciences and remain constantly subject to attack.[3] One should be able to look to government at all levels for more substantial investment and to industry as it increasingly recognizes not only its social responsibility but its larger self-interest as well. One should also be able to anticipate greater in-

[3] As of 1964, the psychological and social sciences were receiving from the federal government only 4 per cent of the support for research and development that was devoted to all research fields. The physical sciences received 74 per cent and the life sciences 21 per cent of the total of 5.78 billion dollars. Carl Pfaffman, "Behavioral Sciences," in *Basic Research and National Goals*, p. 228. In 1967, the level of federal research expenditures in the welfare area was .2 *per cent* of federal welfare program expenditures.

volvement from foundations and non-profit organizations of all kinds and from the universities.

Within the universities, the schools of social work occupy a particularly appropriate position from which to be influential in such developments, together with other professional schools, academic departments, and communal institutions. Secretary John W. Gardner addressed himself to this subject, in part, in his remarks to the Annual Program Meeting of the Council on Social Work Education in 1966. Speaking of his vision of the school of social work of the future, he said:

Like all of the great professional schools of 1990, it will have extremely close ties with the basic fields of science and scholarship in the university—in this case, with the behavioral and social science fields. Indeed it will not be ranked as a distinguished school of social work unless it is associated with an institution in which those fields are strong. . . .

One aspect of the relationship will be much more highly developed than it is today, and that is the provision for innovation. Long before 1990, the behavioral and social science fields in the university, the schools of social work and the social agencies will have joined forces to provide far better arrangements than now exist for the continuous renewal of the field. The basic scientific and scholarly fields will be in sufficiently close touch with current practice so that their traditional function of supplying new knowledge, ideas, and criticism will be characterized by heightened relevance to social problems at hand. The schools of social work will work closely with social agencies in developing new applications of the basic ideas and testing them in practice. Through the close collaboration of the three institutions, innovations will move easily from idea to plan to pilot-testing to general acceptance (or rejection if unsound).[4]

The School of Applied Social Sciences of Case Western Reserve University had decided to celebrate its fiftieth anniversary with a colloquium on the theme of social theory and social invention, "The translation of ideas and knowledge into action for the welfare of society," and did so very much in the spirit of Secretary Gardner's remarks. The selection of this theme in part reaffirmed in today's terms the hope of the School's founders, who wished to organize a professional school of social work wherein the social sciences

[4] "Remarks by John W. Gardner," in *Journal of Education for Social Work,* Vol. II, No. 1 (Spring, 1966), p. 7.

would be drawn upon for direct application to the needs of society. It symbolized as well the School's view of an expanded function for social work education, as well as serving to direct the attention of social scientists to the pivotal issue of the contribution of social science theory to the well-being of society.

In the papers addressed to this theme, Gunnar Myrdal takes a guarded and somewhat pessimistic position on the impact of the social sciences on society. He states that they have advanced more slowly than have the natural sciences partly because the great thinkers of the past generation or two have gone into the natural sciences, so that there has been, in effect, a maldistribution of intellectual brilliance between the two. He stresses, too, the greater difficulty in attacking the problems of social science, because such problems cannot be attacked by abstract manipulation of constants and variables. The constraints on translating theory into action are more strongly imposed in the social sciences because there is no agreement as to the truth of a discovery on the part of either professionals or lay people. Myrdal goes on to take American social scientists to task for having been derelict in their duty to educate and to urge action on the part of the public in areas of vital national concern; but he tempers his criticism by noting that the "escapist scientism rampant in domestic issues" has been discarded in foreign policy matters, where the academic community has made a contribution.

The three social economists commenting on Myrdal's statement all take issue with him in one way or another. Julia Henderson emphasizes that social scientists are making a major contribution to the thinking that is going into the policy-making processes in United Nations agencies, as well as in national governments in such areas as urbanization. She also expresses more optimism than is communicated by Myrdal about the attraction of talented young people to careers in the social sciences and to the applied social science fields. George Rohrlich concentrates on the theme of training social work professionals in social policy and reinforces Myrdal's point about the importance of reawakening among social scientists a sustained interest in critical social problems. Eveline Burns disagrees with Myrdal about the influence of social scientists and considers such influence to be greater than he would concede. She points to the effects on national policies of the work of Keynes and of Myrdal himself, as well as that of the demographers, whose contribution has led to the preoccupation of politicians, professionals, and technicians in many fields with the population explosion.

Charles Frankel accepts the premise that social theory has lagged behind social invention. He presents several classic philosophical points of view contributing to the examination of their relationship. Platonism sets up an abstract morality to which all action is to be related. Conservatism emphasizes the relationship to tradition. Historicism postulates a general dynamic of history within which one may formulate and test social theory. Finally, "piecemeal social engineering" is presented as a point of view where *ad hoc* efforts are attempted in order to change unacceptable conditions, without reference to any large-scale theories. Frankel notes both the contributions and the weaknesses in each of these theoretical positions and the consequences derived from their premises. He concludes that we are suffering not from too much, but from too little, ideology— too few choices from among different systems for translating ideas and principles into action.

The commentators on Dr. Frankel's paper all come from the fields of social welfare and social work education. Dame Eileen Younghusband concludes that "the reasons for action come down in the end to value judgments and motivation." She stresses the importance of increasing our knowledge about how to motivate people and enhance the education of professionals in order to help bridge the gap between theory and practice. Dean Schottland notes that social work has never, in fact, had a philosophy that has been agreed upon but at different times has embraced each of the four philosophical positions that Frankel outlines. He considers "piecemeal engineering" to be the characteristic approach currently but expresses the hope that it will be replaced increasingly by rational social planning based on ideological positions. Whitney Young, Jr., takes issue with Frankel particularly in his interpretation of Frankel's position that reform would be undertaken only on those issues that did not arouse deep-seated moral disagreements. There, Young affirms, one ignores the constructive role that conflict may have in the resolution of critical social issues.

Melvin Tumin deals with a central issue in social theory bearing on social policy. He concentrates on the distribution of power, which he defines as the capacity to realize one's own ends, even against opposition. In power relationships Tumin sees a crucial determinant in both the form and content of human relationships generally. He develops the concept of "captives" as referring to those who are compelled to serve the ends of others more powerful. When more power is acquired by captive groups, they may turn on their benefactors or develop increasing discontent because of new awareness of gaps between themselves and the more powerful. New balances of power, however, are being arrived at constantly and should be accepted by the former "captors" quite pragmatically, because the former "captives" will not permit a return to any previous state of passive submission. Moreover, from the point of view of social philosophy, one may take the position that greater social harmony may exist with compliance, conformity, and consent as modes of acquiescence, and Tumin argues the case for greater sharing of power in order to make healthy consent the norm, with consequences in more rewarding relationships for both the more and the less powerful.

All three discussants take issue with some elements of Tumin's approach. Irving Rosow develops the theme that inequality of power is not bad per se, that there are positive aspects in unequal power that make for co-ordination of complex social processes, provide desirable role models, and limit destructive conflict. Unequal power is harmful if it is exercised on the premise that might makes right, if it degrades others, or if it is based simply on economic dominance. Lucien Mehl also argues that inequality of power is not necessarily bad, that the same people may be captors or captives in different situations. This, he feels, is not necessarily unhealthy, and tensions are necessary for progress both within society and within the family, which Tumin identifies as one context in which different power relationships prevail. Eugen Pusić refers to power as instrumental rather than as a kind of instinctual or primordial drive. He feels that Tumin's concept of power is incomplete. One should add to it the need for motivation for continuing exercise of power by the captors, as well as the provision of a rationale for explaining continuing submission by the captives.

Michael Harrington explores the philosophy of present-day American society and the federal government. He tackles the concept of "the Great Society" and dismisses it as rhetoric concerned with "windy futurism." He develops the theme that "the profit motive can no longer be regarded as the keystone of economics and the test of patriotism" and observes that, if this premise is adopted and given reality by the development of a social accounting system, then one may begin to approach the Great Society as a possible reality. At present, because of the absence of strong counter-measures, both the disbursement of federal funds and the general tax structure tend to benefit the upper and middle classes at the expense of the poor in society. These inequities can be remedied by the application of social accounting principles to both spending and taxing. He looks to the deep currents against materialism among the best educated of American youth as a vital source in stimulating necessary conflict and consequent institutional changes.

Alton Linford points out in his discussion that many social policy decisions must be made without adequate data, and there is, as yet, insufficient knowledge to provide sound input data for effective social accounting. Richard A. Cloward delivers a hard-hitting attack on Harrington's general position by arguing that social accounting will be seriously compromised as an effective technique for improving the conditions of the least powerful and poorest in American society, because those administering a social accounting system will not represent the poor. The central problem, he maintains, is to enable the poor to gain some influence over powerful governmental bureaucracy, including those who would direct the social accounting process. John B. Turner refers to "the revolution" proposed by Michael Harrington as benign, since both the "ins" and "outs" are expected to co-operate. He, too, indicates that the poor should develop functional power.

Repeatedly in these discussions, commentators from, or close to, the field of social work education stress that it is important for schools of social work (as well as social scientists) to become more involved in broad-scale social problems, to become more invested in the relationship of social theory to social application, and to develop programs that would prepare professionals to deal more effectively with issues of social policy. These emphases are congenial to today's mood in social work and social work education, although efforts to move vigorously in these directions still are not developed fully.

The intent of the colloquium, however, and the implications of the theme that is addressed go considerably beyond the interests of social work or, for that matter, the concerns of social scientists. The subject is of vital national concern, for the underlying motif is that, as a society, we have not been making adequate use of social science theory already developed; and, despite the fact that our quantitative investment in social science research and application is larger than that of other countries, the relative investment compared to other fields of research, as indicated, is minor.[5] The discussion raises the question of whether we are, indeed, in need of a new breed of professional, with one foot in theory and the other in application, whose preoccupation would center on the extraction of meaning from theory, and its translation into policies and programs.

A recent illustration of such a translation on the national level was the development of the Operation Head Start program from a relatively small-scale intensive experiment, to determine under what conditions young children who otherwise might be expected to do poorly in school might improve their learning potential. Indeed, the programmatic translation was perhaps developed before all of the theoretical and experimental work could be concluded; yet it has thus far proven to be one of the more acceptable and effective of the antipoverty programs.

Translation into practice tends to be easier in fields drawing on psychological, rather than on sociological or anthropological, approaches. The applications of learning theory to educational processes have become rapid. Such applications, however, tend to be within areas where value conflicts and strong political positions are

---

[5] A report on social research needs in Great Britain argues for the rapid expansion of government and private foundation support for research in the social sciences in England and for sharply increased output of research workers as matters of national policy requirements. "A change of the order envisaged will take place only if there is a conviction that improved solutions to many important problems now facing Great Britain require the contribution of social sciences. Until recently this conviction has not been widely held. There have been signs, however, that it is coming into existence, and bringing with it an increase in willingness to commit resources." *Social Research and a National Policy for Science* (London: The Tavistock Institute of Human Relations, 1964), p. 3, section 8.

minimal. In fields such as race relations, urban planning, and welfare or housing policy, it is not theoretical work which is drawn upon so much as professional judgment, "common sense," and political choices, subject to technical implementation.

Historical analogies concerning the relationship to technology of the physical and biological sciences, on the other hand, and of the social and behavioral sciences to their technology, on the other, cannot be relied on in all respects as a guide to the development of large-scale applications of social theory. Yet there are lessons to be learned from the experience in the exact sciences. Certain preconditions seem to be necessary for such technological application: (1) the availability of fundamental theory capable of being tested, with scientific consensus as to its validity; (2) society's willingness to concede expertise beyond the level of life experience and common-sense judgment to the social scientist on matters of social consequence; (3) the availability of scientist-professionals devoted to application, capable of building on theory and of seeking creative and significant modes of application; and (4) society's willingness to provide the resources not only for theory development and testing but also for large-scale application. These preconditions are simply another way of identifying some of the major impediments to a release of energies for social invention stemming from social science theory.

First, as Myrdal maintains, there is relatively little fundamental theory in the social field that has been tested and whose validity has been accepted scientifically. The complexity of the testing is one source of difficulty. Moreover, when research evidence cannot be conclusive, different value positions by different social scientists tend to prevent agreement on the soundness of the theory itself.

Second, except for certain aspects of economic theory—and then only tenuously—society is not willing to concede to the social scientist expertise in areas of social judgment beyond that of the layman, whether it is in control of deviant behavior, social arrangements of public housing, income maintenance systems for the poor, or planning for redistribution of power and greater stability in the inner cities. These are defined as value questions whose answers are to be determined by economic considerations and by political process through mediating conflict between different interest groups. Such processes and competing value positions will, of course, prevail under any circumstances, but the options toward which such processes are directed can be much broader and more far reaching when they derive from systematic application of theory rather than from *ad hoc* collections of either lay or technical judgment. Moreover, the technological implementation of these choices in the scientific area is not a matter of value questions to be determined politically.

It is the political process which ultimately decides our objectives in space technology and where and to what extent society's investments in this field will go. It is not through political process, however, that society decides what kind of space technology should be developed or from what scientific knowledge such technology should be derived. It leaves such determination to scientific bodies. This is not so in the social field. Whether because social scientists themselves do not agree on the merits of given theory or on the direction of the necessary technology or on value positions, or because they have not aggressively staked their claims for competence in the social field, or because social issues are not defined by the public as being amenable to scientific approaches, society does not accord the social scientist—and here I would include the social worker to the extent that he is an applied social scientist—authority comparable to that of the natural scientist.

The growth of natural science as science became most seminal at the points where "common sense" was left behind and theoretical investigation proceeded on scientific routes that led to formulations well beyond what any "practical experience" or "sound human judgment" could possibly envision, whether it was in the field of cellular structure, the nature of viruses, or the atmosphere of the planets. In the social field, each citizen is his own expert. To this reluctance to accept scientific expertise comparable to that accorded the natural scientist may be added the apprehension of being manipulated and depersonalized by "social engineering" approaches.

Under these conditions it is understandable that there has not grown up a significant cadre of social and behavioral scientists primarily concerned with problems of application of theory. The scientist is generally preoccupied with the pursuit of knowledge and the testing and development of theory but not characteristically—

although there are many exceptions—with large-scale application of programs in the social field. Those in the applied fields, on the other hand, are rarely in positions to initiate programs for field-testing of potential social inventions stemming from scientific foundations. Their energies are fully occupied in coping with current problems through existing programs and techniques, although action-oriented professionals attempt to apply those theoretical concepts made available that can be redefined in action terms—for example, in the utilization of anomie theory in dealing with deviant behavior, or in the planning of programs of community mental health. There remains a large gap, however, between the world of social science and the world of translation into policy and program. The efforts to close this gap by social scientists primarily concerned with affecting social policy (such as their contribution to the historic Supreme Court decision of 1954 on school segregation) and the efforts of professional practitioners to become more knowledgeable about theoretical contributions that can be put to use are still too insufficient for the purposes of American society.

The resources are not provided in any comparable way for theory development and testing in the social sciences as they are in the physical and biological sciences, much less for research in application. There is neither the equivalent of the industrial laboratory—except perhaps for the social agencies, whose latitude for basic innovation and field-testing is restricted—nor, as yet, the readiness of government to commit anywhere nearly comparable resources.

All of these impediments are interrelated. They speak to the necessity for the development of more theory, for more concern with translation of such theory into use, and for larger allocations of resources to the needs of such translation. Such progress will not resolve the value dilemmas within society and among social scientists, but it should provide a wider range of options from which to select in pursuing and making more real those values which prevail.

Social scientists are not necessarily in the best position to extract inventions from the theories they hope to develop and test, just as physicists are not necessarily the best engineers. In order to build stronger bridges between theory and application, new roles will have to be developed combining those of the scientist and the professional. Gradually, slowly, a new breed is indeed emerging, in the social and behavioral sciences and in social work, that is concerned with the translation of theory into technology and action. It will take far greater investments in education, however, and far larger allocation of resources for social research purposes than we have been accustomed to, by government, universities, and community facilities, to produce results worth being termed social inventions based on theory.

As the participants in this colloquium have in diverse ways emphasized, social work education has special obligations and opportunities in furthering the development of these objectives. The schools of social work can enable their faculties and students, and so the world of practice, to reduce the gap between knowing and doing, to spur creative translation of theory into application, to define the essence of our social problems and the value positions upon which social technology could be based, and to collaborate more closely with other professions and disciplines toward increasingly effective means of preventing and resolving our social ills and strengthening the well-being of our people. There is a crying need for new ideas and new approaches not only to meet today's requirements but to prepare for tomorrow's. The relevance of social science and those who draw on it professionally to our country's and the world's problems is being put to the test; so is our society's willingness to enhance such relevance by greatly strengthened encouragement and support.

Contents

III

IV

I

THE ESSAY

The Relation of Theory to Practice: Some Standard Views

CHARLES FRANKEL
Assistant Secretary of State for Educational and Cultural Affairs

COMMENTARY

CHARLES I. SCHOTTLAND
Dean, The Florence Heller Graduate School for Advanced Studies in Social Welfare, Brandeis University

DAME EILEEN L. YOUNGHUSBAND
Advisor, National Institute for Social Work Training (London); President, International Association of Schools of Social Work

WHITNEY M. YOUNG, JR.
Executive Director, National Urban League, Inc.

THE RESPONSE

CHARLES FRANKEL

The Relation of Theory to Practice: Some Standard Views

CHARLES FRANKEL

It was noted by Plato that it is easier to teach a slave boy geometry than it is to teach the sons of Pericles wisdom. A similar thought has occurred to countless observers since. The difference between man's knowledge and mastery of the physical world and his knowledge and mastery of himself is enormous and embarrassing. Another fact, however, is equally interesting. Not only does social theory lag behind physical theory; social theory also lags behind social invention.

Modern life is in large part the work of a remarkable series of ingenious and original devices for either controlling or rationalizing social relations and for either distributing or mitigating the risks of human life. A random list of such devices illustrates the point: the clock, insurance, double-entry bookkeeping, the limited liability corporation, Roberts' Rules of Order, federalism as a political system. Indeed, the social inventiveness of man has probably had far more to do with our present state of well- or ill-being than any social theories we have accumulated.

Consider, for example, the relationship to social action of two bodies of social theory that have preoccupied the twentieth century. In this century, men have placed large bets on the social theory of Marx and the psychological theory of Freud, and have been willing to undo and redo inherited modes of conduct on the assumption that these theories are true. Yet their actual relationship to the social innovations introduced in their name is ambiguous.

The ideas of Freud and Marx have had a heuristic value, suggesting avenues for inquiry and emphases for social action. They have provided their believers with an intellectual rationale, allowing

3

them to explain and justify what they do. And they have undoubtedly presented us with broad insights useful in understanding human life. But they do not have the same relationship to social inventions introduced in their name that the ideas of Newton have to the adventures of the astronauts or that chemistry has to chemical fertilizers. The applications of the social theories of Freud and Marx cannot be shown to be the precise, unequivocal, and logical derivations of these theories. And this fault is not limited to just these two theories. Most social theories, past and present, have been ambiguously related at best to what men have actually done.

Why does social invention appear to remain more independent of social theory today than physical invention of physical theory? Is the situation curable, or are we dealing simply with original sin, with the facts of man's stubbornness, and his incapacity to be objective about himself? Indeed, should we try to cure this situation? Is it conceivable that we are better off depending, on the one side, on tradition and common sense, and, on the other, on hunch and ingenuity?

There is, obviously, a considerable difference between physical and social theory because physical events can be subjected to controlled manipulation whereas human moral codes—and human resistance to being manipulated—impose limits on social experimentation. However, statistical techniques, refined survey procedures, pilot studies and the like have reduced this difference considerably. The question remains, therefore, why such methods have not led to greater success in the building or testing of social ideas at the basic theoretical level. It is a question that can be approached from a number of points of view. There are psychological and sociological reasons for the gap between social theory and social practice. There are political reasons and economic obstacles. There are the difficulties inherent simply in the extraordinarily complex process of translating social policies into coherent programs of action for giant bureaucracies and large and heterogeneous governments and societies. But there are also certain deeply embedded points of view that affect men's thoughts about the relationship that is proper between social theory and social invention, and these points of view also have a bearing on the matter. In this paper I wish to survey some of the best known and most influential of these, and to see in what ways they illuminate this relationship and in what ways they mislead us about it.

I. The Platonic View

There is much in Plato's philosophy that can be accepted by only a few today. There is much in it, indeed, at which he himself appears to have smiled. Side by side with his social idealism and his faith in philosophical reason, Plato's philosophy contains ironical commentaries on the fate of both idealism and reason in the everyday world of politics and illusion. Nevertheless, if we do not cling too closely to the letter of Plato's argument, a conception of the nature of social theory and of its proper relation to social invention can be stated to which it is appropriate to attach Plato's name as a symbol. This Platonic view has had enormous appeal and continues to exercise much greater influence than is supposed.

In essence, this Platonic view holds that the central object of social theory is to specify the Good for man, and that the statement of such an ideal is the indispensable prelude to any program for social reform. Moreover, when we think about such an ideal we should not let our minds be sullied by merely practical considerations—for example, that there may be no great popular sentiment for what we discover to be the ideal Good. Such considerations, according to the Platonic view, are merely circumstantial; the views of *hoi polloi* have nothing to do with what is right or wrong from a rational point of view.

Indeed, a rational idea of the Good will incorporate within it all moral principles that have any claim to man's rational assent. A plurality of competing moral codes, each with its own legitimacy, is logically inconceivable. A Good Society, therefore, cannot be a compromise among disparate interests or points of view. The entire society will be consistent with some single, logically interconnected set of principles. And social invention, accordingly, consists simply in developing the practical strategy to realize this antecedent blueprint of a Good Society. Platonism begins the work of rational social control by determining how things should be. It does not develop its blueprint for reform by looking, first, at the actual terrain and materials with which one has to work.

It would take us too far from the main point of the present meeting to discuss the difficulties of this Platonic view in detail. A schematic statement of a few of its more important defects will indicate the issues that it raises.

(1) A Platonic approach has to establish the exclusive validity of the specific idea of the Good it espouses. If the same special revelation is not accepted by everyone, if no basic axiom is accepted as immediately self-evident, other grounds have to be found, and these inevitably require some form of appeal to observation and experience. But since the Platonist wants to distinguish sharply between what *is* and what *ought to be*, and does not wish to take into account merely accidental circumstances of human life (such as the complex of superstitions and special interests that may happen to prevail at a given time), he has to find some way of distinguishing between the "essential" and the "accidental" in human nature and society. If he can do this, he can then give reasons why the ideal Good he espouses represents the only true fulfillment of man's nature.

This is, in fact, the process of argument which is at the heart of what is known as "Natural-Law" theory. But its logical defect is fundamental—terms like "essential" or "accidental" are relative terms whose meaning can be specified only within a definite frame of reference. It is true to say that oxygen is "essential" only if we accept the maintenance of life as an end. It is true to say that every action "essentially" implies an equal reaction, but only within the framework of Newton's laws. When the Platonist declares, therefore, that something in human nature or society is "essential," he asks us implicitly either to accept the validity of an antecedent ideal, or to accept a general theory of human nature or society. But the first alternative renders his argument circular, and the second renders his argument morally neutral. In any case, it does not answer the question why we should accept as "essential" the particular theory espoused rather than another couched in different terms. For we can theorize about man in economic terms, anthropological terms, psychoanalytic terms, etc., but we have no final embracing theory to which all these separate theories can be reduced unless it is one that is based on faith.

(2) On a more practical level, a basic "problem of transition" is written into the Platonic view. A new order, modeled after a rational idea of the Good, would be one in which all men, or at least those holding key positions in society, recognized and accepted this idea. But to build such an order requires precisely that all men, or at least those holding key positions in society, recognize and accept this idea. In short, for the Platonic view, the means for the achievement of the end already presuppose that the end has been achieved. We must have a perfect world in order to build a perfect world.

Essentially the same problem can be put in another way. The characteristic rejoinder of the Platonist to the argument that a rational society cannot be created because men are irrational is that human irrationality is the product of irrational social arrangements. The object of Platonic social reform is to liberate man, to build a new man or a new human nature. Unfortunately, however, we have to assume that those who will superintend this process are already rational men, since they know quite truly and accurately what the rational ends of human social existence are. And such men will apparently exist despite the corrupt society in which they grew up. In short, some sort of radical break in what is taken to be the normal chain of cause and effect has to be assumed. Put more briefly, the Platonic strategy of action rests on a faith in miracles. As a result, Platonism in social action has frequently tended to turn into something quite different. On one side, it ascends from social activism into essentially religious emotions such as continued hope despite all broken hopes. On the other side, it descends from activism into purely verbal and ideological rehearsals of the great day that is to come, thus giving its adherents their reward by allowing them to dwell on the beauty of their theories rather than by changing anything that exists.

(3) Accordingly, Platonism as a strategy of practical reform is rarely in fact what it sets out to be in theory. Confronted by "the problem of transition" that has been described, one response is to admit that the Good Society is an abstract ideal, which cannot be realized in this world, and to withdraw from the world to contemplate this ideal. (This is the classic response of contemplatives.) A

second response is to say that the ideal is of practical use simply as a negative instrument of criticism which tells us what is wrong even though it does not tell us what to do about it. (This is the classic response of many intellectuals.) A third is to divide the world into two spheres, the ideal and the practical, and to hold that a separate morality applies to each. (This is almost every practical man's response, and reveals his crypto-Platonism.) This espousal of the need for a "second-best morality" turns Platonism on its head. A view which begins by asserting that truly successful action must be guided by a commitment to ultimate principles ends by saying that we must ignore our ultimate principles if we are to act successfully. The Platonic view has been, in fact, a major influence on the attitudes with which both intellectuals and practical men have approached the relation of social theory to social action. It helps explain why theory and practice have been kept in separate compartments.

Yet the Platonic view has had this influence because it also responds to certain facts about the relation of ideas to practice. First of all, in spite of its perfectionist and other-worldly outlook—indeed, *because* of this outlook—the Platonic view is immensely practical. On the field of social combat, it has beaten self-styled "practical" points of view more often than not. The passion that comes from living for an ideal and organizing all one's life around it is a very powerful passion. It is a vital part of politics; tough-minded, empirical politicians ignore it at their peril. Indeed, they often end in the same tender-minded position as the Platonist—pleading, against all the evidences of human folly, that men be reasonable. It is only that they mean by human folly the Platonic mania for the ideal, the Platonic desire to be wholly rational.

More fundamentally still, Platonism puts its finger on an essential condition for the translation of social theory into social action. It makes it plain that such a translation logically presupposes a moral or social ideal. The wholeheartedly practical man is impractical in the simple sense that, as he tinkers here and compromises there, he cannot say what all his practice adds up to. The Platonic view has exercised its appeal because it appears to state what must be stated if social action deserves to be called rational. It says what the action is all about. It states an ultimate objective. It defines, or at least tries to define, the good society.

II. The Conservative View

At the other pole from the Platonic view is what may be called "the conservative view." A brief summary will not do entire justice to this point of view. Still, allowing for the requirements of brevity, it can, I think, be accurately characterized as follows.

The conservative view holds that human life is too complex to be directed by the human intelligence. Human theories, indeed, are inherently falsifications of reality because they are inevitably abstract and general. They pull facts out of context, overlook the singularity of each individual case, and oversimplify the entire problem of acting in the world. It is not theory, therefore, which should be used to give guidance to human affairs but inherited tradition, which is steeped in the realities of human life. For human action is unintelligible except as the product of inherited tradition. People behave as they do for no reason more abstruse or complicated than simply that they have inherited these ways of behaving. And if we try to break this mold of tradition, we break people loose from the only effective controls over their behavior.

From the point of view of the systematic conservative, therefore, the proper aim of social action is simply to avoid having any large, supervening aim. The aim of social action is just to keep going, which is quite difficult enough in itself. If we ask, with the Platonist, where we are going, we merely ask a question that rocks the boat, and that every sensible man knows cannot be answered. For the single surest prediction we can make about the human scene is that the consequences of human plans are unpredictable. From this point of view, there is a place for innovation and invention, but a limited place. We resort to them when there is a need to patch up some tear in tradition or to find some way of adjusting tradition to new circumstances. But we ought never to introduce a change just because a theory calls for one. And when we do take action we should trust our inherited intuitions about right and wrong and not an abstract plan.

That this point of view has defects has been pointed out by numerous observers.

(1) The conservative approach assumes that the tradition of a society is a unitary and internally harmonious whole. This approach

is therefore of no use when, as is usually the case, there are conflicting traditions—for example, the tradition in the United States that all men are created free and equal, and the tradition that Negroes deserve to be kept in an inferior place. Under such circumstances, we need an independent moral principle to determine which tradition is worthy of our loyalty. Indeed, the assumption that a society's tradition is internally consistent logically presupposes the availability of some principle with respect to which it can be said that everything is consistent with everything else. Accordingly, a "tradition" becomes the embodiment of an idea. The conservative is actually a Platonist in spite of himself.

(2) The conservative's reminder that we cannot predict all the consequences of human actions cuts both ways. Neither can we predict the consequences of human inactions. The conservative's fear of taking a chance on ideas is peculiarly inappropriate in times of rapid change, when radical choices must be made even if the only desire is to preserve what is valuable from the past. To allow things to drift does not ensure, after all, the survival of what we prize.

(3) The conservative's attack on "theories," far from being realistic, represents a rejection of the human condition. Human theories are admittedly abstract, which is precisely why they are valuable to us. The fact that a map is abstract, and is not a duplicate of the terrain to which it refers, is the reason why it gives us guidance. Whether we are conservatives or not, we use ideas, either inherited ones or new ones. If they are oversimplifications, we shall make mistakes. But the problem is to find ideas that are not oversimplifications; the problem is not to avoid ideas. And common-sense intuitions, after all, may also be oversimplifications, not to mention the fact that one man's intuitions are very often another man's poison.

(4) Finally, once the conservative grants that invention and innovation sometimes have a place, the fat is in the fire. The question becomes that of determining when to innovate, and how much, and in what way—questions that cannot be answered by appealing to tradition, but only by assessing the nature and magnitude of the problem confronted.

Unfortunately, while we can agree with the conservative that, other things being equal, the smaller a change is the better it is, this axiom tells us very little. In a modern, technological society, where innovation is itself a tradition and the consequences of innovation are far-reaching, it tells us less than nothing. For, on one side, we are warned by the conservative not to introduce changes that represent deliberate efforts to remodel society, while, on the other side, he does not tell us what to do about innovations like atomic power or television that are introduced without a deliberate social aim but whose social consequences undermine many received modes of conduct. The pragmatic meaning of conservatism in a technological society is that we are permitted to be inventive about everything but the social control of the consequences of our inventiveness. Of course, the conservative may decide that it is necessary to resist or limit technological innovation because it is socially disturbing. If he adopts this line, however, he will no longer be a conservative, but will be involved in radical forms of social engineering.

Still, the conservative approach has survived because, like the Platonic view, it has something useful to say. It points to certain fundamental facts about the relation of theory to practice. The first of these facts is a psychological fact about human beings: we are all more traditional than we know. To make changes we begin, inevitably, with where we are and what we have been; and where we are and what we have been have a more important influence than anything else on where we can go. Proposals for social change that do not take this fact into account are bound to lead to disappointment or self-deception.

A second insight of conservatism has to do with the logical relationship between abstract ideals and practical decisions to act upon them in a specific context. No abstract ideal—whether we think of "democracy," "equality," "welfare" or any other—tells us by itself what should be done in a concrete case. It needs to be interpreted. There have to be rules that tell us how and where to apply it. When we apply the general maxim that killing other human beings is wrong, for example, we employ certain unspoken rules that exempt, say, killing in war, or abortion for medical reasons, or self-defense. In employing the ideal of equality, to take another example, we normally recognize that equality is not incompatible with choosing some people to be the leaders of others, or with paying certain categories of workers more than we pay others.

This process of implicit interpretation and restriction is necessary in relation to all abstract principles. Otherwise they would be empty formulae, like algebraic equations. And as the examples I have given suggest, the principles of interpretation which we use are often implicit and unconscious. They are supplied by the "common sense" and habitual modes of behavior of a society, and are usually just taken for granted. In practice, therefore, all social ideals have a large element of simple, brute tradition in them; and we do not discover all that we presuppose about them except in the actual process of putting them into effect. The idea of remaking a society *de novo*, therefore, is a delusion. The application of theory to practice inevitably involves reliance on the cake of custom. The conservative may embrace this truth with more passion than the rest of us, but he is not wrong to think it a truth.

III. The Historicist Approach

During the nineteenth century an influential body of doctrine about the relation of social theory to social invention emerged which has since come to be known as "historicism." Major figures of the nineteenth century—Hegel, Comte, Spencer, and, most conspicuously, Marx—developed historicist doctrines in one form or another. Historicism has formidable antagonists today, but its continuing influence in the world at large is also too evident to need to be argued.

Although there are different versions of historicism, all have certain common characteristics. Historicism holds that there is a law of history in accordance with which the historical process as a whole tends to move in a certain general direction. The social problems that arise in the course of history are simply instances of "cultural lag," arising because development in one sphere (for example, technology) is out of tempo with development in another sphere (for example, property relations). The solution of a social problem consists, therefore, in rectifying this kind of historical discordance. The rectification may occur with conscious human intervention or without it, but in either case the essential point is that human beings should not try to impose their own external preference or goals, but should determine what the basic direction of change is and move along with it.

Thus, in contrast with Platonists, historicists characteristically deny that they have any blueprints for the future. Marx, for example, scoffed at utopian socialists. His writings are devoted almost exclusively to the evolution and breakdown of capitalism, and when he speaks of "socialism" he does so only in the sketchiest terms. "Theory," for the historicist, consists of general laws from which the direction of historical change can be deduced. Effective practice consists in conforming to these laws. In contrast with Platonism, which believes that a theory of ends should be primary, historicism concentrates on a theory of the means, and downgrades the discussion of ends.

Historicism has been so thoroughly discussed that there is little point in debating its merits at length here. Its two most obvious defects can be indicated fairly briefly.

(1) Historicism asks us to accept the view that moral judgment consists simply in picking the winning side. But lost causes are not the nobler for being lost, and victorious causes do not become nobler for being victorious.

(2) Historicism assumes that it is possible to speak intelligibly of general laws of history. Undoubtedly, there are general laws which can be employed to explain historical events. That Napoleon's ambitions grew with success is something we can understand, for example, in terms of human psychology. But we cannot deduce Napoleon's invasion of Russia from this abstract knowledge. We also have to know where Russia is on the map, and this is a brute fact independent of the general laws of human psychology which we apply to Napoleon's behavior. A law of history which would allow us to speak of a necessary direction of change for the historical process as a whole requires us to suppose that all the circumstances of history constitute a logically interrelated whole, and that no event is accidental or logically independent of any other. This supposition cannot be defended.

On the contrary, at any given time, there is always, as a matter of fact, more than one significant and powerful trend of change. In the United States today, for example, the urbanization of society has brought greater centralization of power in government and communications. At the same time, developments in computers and in information storage and transmission permit greater decentralization of decision-making authority. Indeed, one and the same trend usually has plural implications. Urbanization means more legal and administrative regulation of life; it also means more personal privacy and freedom. Human choice and ingenuity with regard to the future therefore remain decisive.

These considerable defects of the historicist approach should not cause us to ignore, however, the ways in which historicism clarifies the relationship between social theory and social invention. We need not believe in an inevitable law of history in order to recognize that, in a given epoch, certain broad trends of change are dominant and cannot easily be reversed. And we need not accept the brutal view that justice is what the victors in history say it is to recognize that human moral standards are condemned to impotence unless they are framed in terms that make it possible to act upon them with some hope of success.

The historicist view, in short, calls attention to the context in which attempts at social invention take place. At any particular time, only certain choices are open. Even when men have freedom and their ideals affect what happens, their freedom is, nevertheless, limited, and their hopes frustrated—unless these hopes are historically relevant. To translate theory into action we need more, accordingly, than general theories about human nature or society, and more than close empirical knowledge of limited ranges of fact. We need to be aware of the more important dynamics of change and the probable evolution of controlling institutions and social attitudes. Without such awareness, social theory remains just theory and social inventiveness becomes an exercise in gimmickry.

Historicism, undogmatically interpreted, provides a general approach to the analysis of social problems the value of which persists after we discard historicist pretentions. The concept of "cultural lag," when translated into a methodology of inquiry, becomes the "functionalist" approach. It invites us to explain human habits and institutions in terms of the circumstances to which they are responses, and to evaluate them by their effectiveness as responses. To use other language, the historicist view presents each historical situation as a set of problems to be solved. In the long course of human history, the absence of just this general point of view has been the fundamental reason why social theory has not been regularly developed and tested in social practice.

IV. "Piecemeal Social Engineering"

The inherent difficulties of the Platonic, conservative and historicist approaches, and the human troubles they have helped cause or sanction, have led to the increasing influence of another point of view. It is the point of view which is taken, tacitly or explicitly, by a large proportion of those who call themselves "liberal" or "moderate reformers" or "the democratic left." It is espoused, indeed, by a very large number of the new technicians in social research and social action, who would eschew all political labels or distinctions between "Left" and "Right," and who pronounce themselves beyond ideology in their approach to social issues.

One of the most thorough and best known statements of this point of view has been made by Professor Karl Popper, who, towards the end of World War II, gave it the name of "piecemeal social engineering." What "piecemeal social engineering" is *not* is fairly plain. Born out of opposition to other philosophies of politics, it is not Utopian—as Platonism is; it does not distrust rational human efforts to rearrange inherited social institutions—as conservatism does; and it does not assume—as does Marxism—that all problems are of a single piece and that one key unlocks them all. Unfortunately, however, even in Professor Popper's unusually lucid formulation, "piecemeal social engineering" is harder to define in positive terms.

If we hazard such a positive statement, however, we may begin by characterizing "piecemeal social engineering" as the point of view which holds that deliberate social reform is justified and required when some unmistakable and rectifiable social wrong exists. Instead of beginning with a blueprint of *what ought to be*, "piecemeal social engineering" begins where the pain is actually felt, and defines its task as the remedying of the conditions that cause the pain. Thus, abstract arguments about generalized social programs are avoided. For we can detect wrong—and know that it is wrong— much more easily than we can agree on any abstract ideal. We need only show that people are suffering, and that this suffering is avoidable. In brief, social engineering takes its point of departure in a practical consensus, and consists in dealing with definite problems, presented by the existence of specific cases of ill-being. Its function is remedial—to eliminate evils, not to realize an antecedent plan for the Good.

Rational social engineering, furthermore, must be piecemeal. No more should be attempted than needs to be attempted in order to eliminate the wrong which is the target of the reform. In Professor Popper's formulation, "Blueprints for piecemeal social engineering are comparatively simple. They are blueprints for single institutions, for health and unemployment insurance, for instance, or arbitration courts, or antidepression budgeting or educational reform. If they go wrong, the damage is not very great, and a readjustment not very difficult. They are less risky, and for this reason less controversial." [1]

Finally, the distinctive instrument of "piecemeal social engineering" is scientific social theory. The function of such theory is to uncover the social laws that allow us to detect the unintended consequences of human actions—the consequences (for example, cyclical unemployment) that follow from what men do, not because such consequences are consciously willed, but because social arrangements exist (for example, the stock market, the price system) that produce these consequences. Through social theory the conditions that produce such unintended consequences can in principle be identified. And social engineering consists in using such theory to change conditions whose consequences are unacceptable.

In one way or another, probably, most of those who are present here at this meeting would accept "piecemeal social engineering" as the doctrine that comes closest to stating their view of the relation of social theory to social action. Certainly, if I were forced, like the ancient teacher Hillel, to state in a single phrase the approach to social action that I myself favor, I would say, "Piecemeal social engineering." But I would have to add immediately that I found the question unfair and my answer uncomfortable. For "piecemeal social engineering" raises, I think, as many questions as it answers.

(1) In the first place, it simplifies the context in which social

---

[1] *The Open Society and Its Enemies* (Princeton, N.J.: Princeton University Press, 1950), p. 156.

theory is applied to social problems. Specifically, it ignores, or greatly underestimates, the facts of life that generate and require moral debate and political competition.

Consider, first, the phrase "avoidable human suffering," which would permit us, if Professor Popper is right, to avoid fruitless ideological debates about the nature of the Good Society. To take a not at all hypothetical example, is the suffering caused by a famine in another country "avoidable"? The answer, despite appearances, is not a straightforward factual answer. If we look only at the resources that lie within the country affected, the answer is likely to be "No." If we extend the boundaries of the problem beyond national frontiers, the answer will be "Yes." But this is to make, at least in part, a moral decision.

Again, is the suffering caused by racial prejudice "avoidable"? The answer is similarly shot through with moral judgments with respect to which there does not exist a consensus. The suffering can be reduced if we can find ways to reduce racial prejudice or control its expression. But such remedial actions *cause* suffering among those who are prejudiced. In deciding to take action, therefore, we are deciding whose suffering we are going to take most seriously. And this sort of social decision goes beyond simple social engineering. In large part, it is the kind of thing that politics is all about. Indeed, "avoidable suffering" is much too narrow a phrase to cover the problems that call for organized social action, particularly in a relatively well-to-do society. Comparatively few people, for example, may actually feel pain at the untidiness of city streets or the destruction of a countryside. But this in itself is the problem. What is at issue is a scheme of values.

In brief, though it seems to be quite different from Platonism, "piecemeal social engineering" suffers in its own way from the same malady. That malady is the hope of avoiding the clashes over value-systems that divide societies and that make the application of scientific methods of social inquiry so difficult. Platonism tries to avoid such clashes by attaining initial agreement about ultimate values. "Piecemeal social engineering" tries to do so by limiting the sphere of reform to problems that do not arouse deep-seated moral disagreements. But both presuppose, in effect, that a condition for the rational resolution of social issues is the absence of important moral disagreements. Both dream, in a word, of a sanitized social scene uncontaminated by politics. In the case of "piecemeal social engineering," to be sure, the malady is milder, but the difference is the difference between a cold and the flu.

Thus, Professor Popper writes: "In favor of his method, the piecemeal engineer can claim that a systematic fight against suffering and injustice and war is more likely to be supported by the approval and agreement of a great number of people than the fight for the establishment of some ideal." [2] But this is true because "suffering" and "injustice" and "war" are actually more abstract and elusive terms than, say, "socialism" or "capitalism." The moment we come down to cases, and debate the means to these broad ends, the old divisions appear. For some people inevitably pay for other people's added increments of welfare, even if the payment is purely immaterial and consists simply in being forced to accept changes that offend their moral standards.

(2) "Piecemeal social engineering," furthermore, invites questions about what is meant by "piecemeal." Professor Popper speaks of the reform of "single institutions," and offers educational reform as an example. But if we are speaking of educational reforms aimed at lifting the aspirations of the so-called "culturally deprived," for example, we are dealing with a problem that touches on the structure of families, neighborhood conditions, racial discrimination, etc. A fairly large "piece" of society becomes involved. And if we are speaking of the kind of educational reform that has been attempted in the last century by nations like France, Russia, Mexico and Turkey—namely, the secularization of education—we are dealing with a problem which arises not within a single institution, but which reflects ideological and moral disagreements affecting all or most institutions in the society. While any sensible man will wish to avoid Utopian or unrealistic approaches to such problems, and while any moderate man will wish to avoid violence and fanaticism in dealing with them, it also seems unrealistic and Utopian to hope, with the piecemeal social engineer, that we can somehow insulate a struggle to reform a single institution from the larger sentiments and hostilities that affect the society more generally.

(3) As these remarks may suggest, "piecemeal social engineering," taken all by itself, presupposes a great deal about the social condi-

[2] *Ibid.*, p. 155.

tions in which it is applied. It presupposes a large degree of cultural homogeneity, fairly stable political arrangements, a large measure of political consensus, and the existence of problems none of which require fundamental changes in the social outlook or traditional prerogatives of those affected. It would seem to apply, where it applies at all, to developed industrial societies where the outlook of most people is already sympathetic to the idea of social innovation guided by scientific methods.

This does not mean that controlled social experimentation is out of place in the developing world. On the contrary, responsible efforts to deal with the problems of these societies should obviously be based, if possible, on the experience gained from pilot projects that are initially small-scale in their scope and limited in the risks they entail. But we cannot speak of "responsible social reform" in such societies if we mean by such reform *ad hoc* and separate efforts to change "single institutions" such as the civil service or the schools.

Such efforts would not be responsible because they would, by hypothesis, overlook the inter-relations of the institutions under reform with many other institutions in the society. Plans for development may be experimental and controlled, but they have to be formulated in such a way that their effects on a broad array of institutions and attitudes are taken into account. Admittedly, holistic planning is Utopian; but social planning, in the context of development, cannot be quite the disjointed affair that "piecemeal social engineering" appears to recommend. Indeed, such planning may be said to have one large over-all purpose—namely, to create conditions and attitudes which will be receptive to the regular translation of social theory into experimental programs of social action.

V. Conclusion

The reader of this examination of some of the standard views of the relation of social theory to social action will be able to construct, if he agrees with what has been said, his own personal schedule of truths and fallacies with regard to this subject. I shall call attention only to those considerations that seem to me particularly worth emphasizing.

(1) Social theory, conceived as a purely *descriptive* matter, must be supplemented by a *philosophical or moral* social theory. The distinction between "descriptive" and "normative" statements is fundamental to the control of scientific inquiry, and it is a mistake to try to identify these two types of theory as one. However, there is no logical basis for moving from descriptive social theory to practical action unless value judgments are made; nor will there be a practical will to action unless these judgments are made explicit. A social philosophy which explores the basic choices available and offers an ordered scheme of preferences for dealing with them is indispensable, therefore, if there is to be a translation of social theory into social action on a scale large enough to fertilize social theory and to affect the social order significantly.

(2) Such a social philosophy, if it serves as the instrument for translating theory into practice, cannot be *a priori* in character. Its tools will be descriptive social theory, broad historical understanding leading to an estimate of the fundamental alternatives available at a given time, and political judgment concerning the possibilities and the costs of different strategies of action. Out of such considerations, such a social philosophy would formulate in an orderly way the key problems to which organized social attention should be directed. Its sketch of a better society would not be a deduction from first principles but an hypothesis, whose validity would be measured by its capacity to inspire and guide remedial action and to solve the problems provoking the action.

(3) Through all this process, fundamental ideals—"equality," "liberty," etc.—play a part. They set the broad boundaries within which a problem is defined, and without them the idea of the "successful solution" of a problem has, in fact, no meaning. But these ideals take on practical meaning only in the process of applying them to specific cases, and in this process of application they are tested and redefined. Accordingly, the application of theory to practice is not simply a process of finding the means for achieving predetermined ends. Neither can it take place, however, by dodging the question of ends and defining "good" simply as the result of a process in which a specific evil has been rectified. The criticism of means requires the criticism of ends, and vice versa. Descriptive social theory is therefore the basic instrument of social philosophy.

But social theory without social philosophy is an incomplete guide to action.

(4) A certain dose of skepticism is desirable with respect to the increasingly popular view that "ideology" is dead. If by "ideology" is meant sterile debates over abstract labels, the death of ideology is "a consummation devoutly to be wished," but it has not yet taken place. If by "ideology" is meant the kind of *a priori* philosophical system which demonstrates that all history and creation stand behind one's own best-loved ideals—the kind of system to which the names of Hegel, Marx and Spencer are attached—we may also hope that ideology is dead, but we are a long way from seeing the fulfillment of this hope. But if by "ideology" is meant a system of guiding ideals and principles of action, we must confess, I think, that we are suffering—in the developed world perhaps most of all— not from too much but from too little "ideology." For one function of ideology is to make explicit the nature of the larger choices that have to be made by a society, together with the broad scheme of preferences required to deal with these choices. In the broad sense, ideology is like philosophy—it clarifies the grounds of choice. It is a necessary instrument of social transition, if that transition can be said to be conscious and deliberate. Admittedly, ideology can exacerbate divisions in a society; it is equally capable, however, of producing new forms of unity. And whether it does the first or the second depends not on anything intrinsic to its abstract function as an ideology, but to its actual content and to the spirit and form of its proposals.

COMMENTARY

CHARLES I. SCHOTTLAND

It is trite to say that we live in an era of change. Yet change is one of the most predominant characteristics of this decade. The universe is being explored, men will soon be walking on the moon, the big computers will increasingly be storing man's knowledge in many areas and releasing it in a systematized fashion upon request, every corner of the globe will be only a short time away by superplanes even now in production—these are merely indicative of the fantastic changes taking place in today's society as our knowledge and mastery of the physical world take specific applied forms.

Our speaker, Charles Frankel, himself represents change, for who would have thought that in 1966 a noted philosopher would be Assistant Secretary of State. Those of us who sometimes despair at the slowness of change in social work ought to be heartened by such a development.

Dr. Frankel's paper on the relation of theory to practice is an excellent, timely, and provocative presentation to those of us engaged in the practice or teaching of social work. Social workers, having divorced the social scientists in the 1920's in order to consummate a marriage with Freud and his disciples, now find the marriage strained, and in reaching for younger romances are embracing the social theories of sociologists, anthropologists, economists, and political scientists. Our effort to understand the nature of our society springs from our hope that we may be able to do something about it. No respectable school of social work today wants to be caught without offerings in social theory. Dr. Frankel has sounded for us a warning signal in pointing out that social theory lags behind social invention. Does this indicate the importance of greater study in our profession to the great social inventions of our time—social insurance, vocational rehabilitation, government financing of housing, public education?

The devastating objectivity with which Dr. Frankel has presented both the affirmative and negative aspects of four philosophical approaches (the Platonic view, the conservative view, the historicist approach, and "piecemeal social engineering") leaves those of us who are not philosophers without a firm philosophical base for our social work practices—but this is a state which is not new to us since social work has never had an agreed-upon social philosophy. Rather we have embraced—or at least certain elements of the social work profession have embraced—each of the four philosophies at some time in our history. Following World War I, social work began to concern itself with the Good Society (the Platonic view) and to ask itself about goals and objectives. Eduard Lindeman propounded such questions—before he too changed his point of view. The conservative view as presented by Dr. Frankel has always been a factor in the development of social work. Sometimes retarding progress, it has nevertheless been a constructive force by enabling us to understand that we must start where we are in order to know where we must go. This has been one of the main tenets of many psychotherapists and has profoundly influenced thought among caseworkers.

Probably social work has had fewer adherents to the historicist approach. With the exception of the Marxists, social work in the United States is dominated by a belief that change can be manipulated—both individual and societal—and that social work can contribute to this change.

It is "piecemeal social engineering" which most accurately characterizes much of social work today, particularly that of those who are engaged in social policy formation and social action. In a sense, this approach has been antagonistic to another social work approach which is based on the theories of Freud. Both theories have produced manifold processes and techniques on the simple assumption that the theories themselves are sound and therefore should be put into practice. Social work has accepted both the unproved theories around psychological individualization and the concepts of "piecemeal social engineering," and has expressed them through social action and social invention.

Dr. Frankel has pointed out (correctly, in my opinion) the limitations of the "piecemeal social engineering" approach. Nevertheless, when forced to make the choice of a single course of social action, he elects this piecemeal approach even though it makes him "uncomfortable." I share the discomfort. His criticism of "piecemeal social engineering" is a criticism of American society as a whole. It is characteristic of the United States that it does not have either clearly enunciated, comprehensive national policies or comprehensive national planning. Such national planning is being attempted in most of the less-developed countries and, of course, in socialist economies. It presents some real difficulties in the complicated and numerous programs of the United States. Just to take a few examples on the Federal government level alone: the Federal government operates or makes funds available for the operation of more than 25 programs providing assistance to persons in locating jobs; there are over 60 Federal programs of financial assistance to individuals and families; there are more than 50 programs of vocational and job training; some 35 programs provide technical guidance and financial assistance in the development of new housing or rehabilitation of existing housing; more than 75 programs have been established to stimulate economic growth, increase employment, and improve the economic environment.

Some of these Federal programs are operated exclusively by the Federal government—such as financial assistance given by the Veterans Administration; some are locally operated with Federal funds going directly from Washington to the local community—such as some programs of the Office of Economic Opportunity; other local programs, such as public assistance, receive Federal funds through the state; still other Federal funds are available for state operated programs—such as public employment offices; even Social Security, long held up as a prime example of efficient Federal administration, now has disability determined by states (for disability insurance) and private carriers (such as Blue Cross) administering Medicare.

These numerous, discrete, and uncoordinated programs make overall planning difficult; in the words of Dr. Frankel, such "holistic planning is Utopian."

However, another factor impedes holistic planning: our inability to enunciate—with any consensus—the value premises from which our goals are derived. I agree with Dr. Frankel that "there is no logical basis . . . for moving to practical action unless value judgments are made," but I feel that his comment that there will not "be a practical will to action unless these judgments are made explicit," while it may be a statement of what *should be*, does not accord with what *is*. As a matter of fact, much successful social action has been carried out by prior agreement on the ends of action by persons who approach the same problem through different or even opposing values; other successful social action has been espoused without any attempt to make value judgments explicit.

Yet those of us engaged in social action frequently feel uncomfortable because of the lack of explicit value goals or judgments as a logical justification for our activities. Fortunately, discussion of values is becoming more dominant in social work circles and is occupying increasing attention by social work practitioners and educators. Of course, most social work values are values held by entire societies in a few cases, by major segments of the population in others, and by only a minority of the population in some areas. The values of social workers, whether explicit or implicit, lead us into conflict with values held by other persons. For example, social workers generally favor abolition of responsibility of children for the financial support of aged parents; this conflicts with a strong, popular belief that adult children owe a duty to their parents (and to society) to support aged, indigent parents. The belief of social workers that public assistance is a "right" and should be available to all on the basis of need, conflicts with widely held beliefs that assistance by government should not be extended to the "unworthy" such as unwed mothers.

Two ideas which I have mentioned from Dr. Frankel's paper, "holistic planning" and "values," need to receive more definitive attention by the social work profession. Both concepts present difficulties in theory and practice. However, we have made considerable progress over the years with reference to both of these concepts. Just consider the philosophical, social, economic, and political distance traveled between the years 1887 to 1954 as illustrated by two pronouncements of two Presidents of the United States. In 1887, President Grover Cleveland vetoed a bill providing for a distribution of seeds to drought-stricken farmers. His veto message acknowledged that "there existed a condition calling for relief" and that a donation of seed "would serve to avert a continuance or return of the unfortunate blight." Nevertheless, President Cleveland felt "obliged to withhold approval of the plan" on the grounds that "I can find no warrant for such an appropriation in the Constitution, and I do not believe that the power and duty of the General Government ought to be extended to the relief of individual suffering. . . ." He urged that such programs should be "steadfastly resisted, to the end that the lesson should be constantly enforced that though the people support the government, the government should not support the people."

In contrast to this, President Dwight D. Eisenhower sent a message to Congress in 1954 which recommended legislation because of the well-established recognition that "The human problems of individual citizens are a proper and important concern of our government ... To help individuals provide (security)—to reduce both the fear and incidence of destitution to a minimum—to promote the confidence of every individual in the future—these are proper aims of all levels of government, including the Federal government."

Or consider the philosophical, legal, political, and social revolution made possible when the Social Security Act was held constitutional and Justice Cardozo declared that "Only a power that is national can serve the interests of all."

Returning to the comment at the beginning of this paper, that change is one of the most predominant characteristics of this decade, one must take note of the fact that there are few eternal values, that values change, and that this constant change makes it difficult to make explicit our values and our guiding ideals and principles. In theory, I agree with Dr. Frankel: we suffer from "too little ideology." In all honesty, however, I must admit participating in social action and avoiding discussion of ideology and values, lest the agreement on the specific action be threatened by disputes over philosophical goals and values by non-philosophers whose values might be governed by visceral rather than rational considerations. In spite of this, I believe with Dr. Frankel that in an era such as the present, where we have many alternative choices, our ideology clarifies the basis of choice and is a necessary instrument for the rational social planning which, hopefully, may someday replace "piecemeal social engineering."

COMMENTARY

DAME EILEEN L. YOUNGHUSBAND

Dr. Frankel's brilliant paper is a salutary reminder that the problems of *where* we want to go and *why* are as pressing as the difficulties of discovering *how* to get there. In addition, he reminds us that the maps made during the last two centuries are no better —if no worse—than a map which is over 2,000 years old.

All four of the social philosophies which Dr. Frankel reviews face the same contrasting dilemmas. On the one hand, starting with a global approach is an insufficient guide to taking the next step, but on the other hand, concentrating solely on next steps cannot be relied upon to add up to a logical, global policy of social action. The latter is indeed a variant of the Benthamite fallacy that each man in pursuing his own self-interest will automatically produce the greatest happiness of the greatest number.

At the same time, Dr. Frankel hints that social theories which start either at the beginning or the end may sometimes meet in the middle and find sufficient common ground for immediate, short-term action even though their fundamental assumptions would ordinarily result in very different long-term policies. We are left, then, with the inevitability of action, but with no agreement about guides to action. At the same time, as Dr. Frankel emphasizes, there are no logical grounds for moving from social theory to social action—and this is the proper sequence of events—save on the basis of value judgments. Here, however, a further difficulty arises in that to a considerable extent most of us don't know what we want but won't be happy till we get it; thus, there are quite profound conflicts in society about what is "good" for people, about what the distribution and use of power should be, and about what incentives to action are most effective. This is probably fortunate. In most societies such conflict prevents any one social theory from being pressed to its logical conclusion as the sole guide to social action.

It is obvious that all practice includes a value judgment of some kind, even on the very grounds for decision that one type of action or social arrangement is to be preferred to others. The value reasons for such preferences may have been examined and may be either adequate or over-simplified; they may or may not be the real reasons for action; or they may be accepted without analysis as self-evident truths. The danger of unexamined or over-simplified value judgments lies in their unintended or unforeseen consequences. Dr. Frankel criticizes the four standard views he examines in terms of certain logical deficiencies. But this leaves open the still more difficult question of the criteria by which we are to judge the "goodness" or "badness" of a philosophy. These criteria are obviously outside the philosophy itself, but we must ask what they are themselves and what validates them.

Men have a tremendous urge to make sense of their experience; indeed, all action is based on some estimate of what makes sense. They do this in many ways, and perhaps philosophy and science are the two most sophisticated forms. Science is now catching up with philosophy—and giving us a tool for the other hand. As Dr. Frankel so cogently urges, our modern problem is to determine how the two hands shall work together, and whether—and in what circumstances—one hand shall or should have mastery over the other.

This issue becomes all the more acute because of the gap, to which Dr. Frankel draws attention, between man's control of the physical world and mastery of himself. As Middleton Murray put it some years ago, we have learned through science and technology to produce a surplus of material goods which we can only give away in hate or in love. So far, our skill at giving them away in hate, through armaments and war, greatly exceeds our ability to give them away in love, through the creation of a world free from squalor, poverty, and ill-health.

This in turn leads on to a further dilemma which is emphasized by Dr. Frankel as being inherent in any social theory other than conservatism. It is the dilemma of how man's innate capacity for attempting to make sense of existence through custom and tradition on the one hand can at the same time be harnessed to his capacity for attempting to make social innovation on the other. The bonding of the two is essential to ensure both continuity of social expectations and appropriate response to the changes introduced by the accelerating, and often one-sided, application of science to human affairs. It is only necessary in this context to mention the new forms of morality called for by the internal combustion engine, or still unsolved problems about the sanctity of human life posed by medicated survival. Science is indeed creating new circumstances in which the right to die deserves as much respect as the right to live.

In societies like our own where individual freedom to choose and to possess is constantly increasing, there is bound to be lopsided development on a scale which we know neither how to control nor how to compensate. Two obvious examples are the population explosion, which is the consequence of myriad individual choices allied with the application of the natural sciences in medicine and agriculture, and the rapid growth of great cities which are unfit to live in. We have also reached a point in the affluent societies where large numbers of people prefer status symbols and conformity to beauty, adventure, and the creative arts. In other words, freedom to choose is assuming no greater importance than freedom to have the same things and do the same things as everyone else in the neighborhood.

The modern dilemma might indeed be called the dilemma of imbalances. This applies alike to the unequal growth of different branches of knowledge, more particularly in the natural as opposed to the social sciences; and, in the application of knowledge, to the crucial consequences which arise from gaps in different branches of knowledge which are interrelated in application but separate at their source; and, finally, to the imbalance of consequences which comes from insufficient wisdom to make sound value judgments in the translation of applied science into social action.

Dr. Frankel would probably say that neither science nor technologies and social inventions can do more than clarify the issues and widen the range of choice. As a last resort, we are forced back on value decisions, and must consider again such fundamentals as the good of the few or the many, re-examine the balance between individualism and collectivism, and decide who should control what for whom—in short, we must define what kind of society we think is a good society.

The reasons for action come down in the end to value judgments and motivation. Thus, the age-old problem—how to equate what we want with what we ought to desire on rational moral grounds —has become more acute in our generation because of the many-sided growth of power which has been generated by science and technology. We may well agree with Dr. Frankel that what we *ought* to desire at any given time should bear some reasonable relation to what is *possible* in the circumstances. (He seems to agree with the English philosopher, T. H. Green, that "what is ethically desirable must be sociologically possible.") I wonder, though, whether we can go the whole way with this point of view. Certain ideals seem to have to undergo a long period of gestation in the human mind before they become sociologically possible. The abolition of slavery is the classic example; others are the still unrealized ideals of the abolition of war and poverty. This nation has embarked on the latter; so far as the former is concerned, it has now become a simple question for all nations of whether we shall abolish war before war abolishes us.

Increasingly, as science makes the attainment of certain ideals technologically possible, we are forced back upon the conflicts and hostilities, the flickering confusion of human motivation, and the enormous force of inertia in human affairs. In our day, it is not only a matter of holding up before ourselves ideals beyond our grasp (like loving our neighbor as ourselves), but also of bridging the gap between what could be achieved and our will to achieve it. That comforting gulf in Thomist philosophy between the law of nature and the law of nations is decreasingly available to us as a means to rationalize our moral turpitudes.

This consideration has two aspects related to the application of social theory to social practice. The first is the necessary increase in our limited knowledge of how to motivate people—motivate more students to learn more, for example. The other is the difficult ethical problems which will arise when we do know how to arouse and direct motivation. Who—and on what grounds—is to make the value choices upon which people should be motivated to act? For example, if we knew as much about motivating people to stop smoking cigarettes as we know about the connection between smoking and lung cancer, would we then be justified in so motivating them?

There is another dimension of knowledge and its application, motivation, and social theory which is worth consideration. It is that the application of science and the application of social wisdom can obviously come only through people, and they simply are not the right size for the task in the absence of social inventions to enlarge them. The useful social devices of the professions (including professional ethics) and related administrative structures and procedures, augmented by technical aids, are helpful means for bridging the gap between knowledge and practice, and, to a more limited extent, between social theory and practice. They are a means indeed for creating the supermen for the more than life-size tasks that modern complexity requires. Professional codes of ethics are also a means for making us more virtuous, reliable, and disinterested in certain aspects of our professional lives than we could realistically be expected to be as private individuals. A crucial link in relating social theory to social practice is the enhancement of professional education, together with better administrative devices and technical aids such as computers.

These various devices are reasonably effective in the middle ranges, but they become decreasingly so at the apex. Here the demand is for people who are larger than life, whether in physical stamina, intellectual grasp, iron nerve, quickness and accuracy of response, moral integrity, or dispassionate compassion. This is obvious enough when we think of heads of state or others in positions of great responsibility. But, we can see it is also just as obviously true in another form, if we reflect on what it takes—by way of personal commitment and scientific detachment—to attempt to reclaim severely damaged and alienated people in our society. In brief, the application of scientific theory, no less than the application of social ethics, will fall far short of what it might be unless we can also devise social inventions that will enable ordinary people to do extra-ordinary things. Plato's philosopher kings are returning in forms to him unknown.

Dr. Frankel has gracefully avoided a head-on collision with that pitfall term "welfare." He points out the limitations of removal of social ills as a comprehensive goal of social action. But all the same, it is very much easier to agree about the desirability of programs to promote education, health, nutrition, crime control and prevention, housing, employment, and social security, than it is to be clear about what are the next stages—unless they be more of the same. While all of these in one way or another promote or protect people's physical well-being, and thus give them the tools with which to fashion independence and happiness, education straddles two worlds. To remove the grosser causes of unhappiness is not to guarantee the effective pursuit of happiness itself— that elusive will o' the wisp which alights on some and eludes others. Indeed, the further we move from negatives to positives, from the body to the mind, from ill health to whatever we mean by positive mental health or well-being, the more misty and the more fraught with disagreement about aims and methods our endeavors become.

We may not agree with the nineteenth-century philosopher Bosanquet that the state cannot actively promote the good life but only "hinder hindrances" to it. But, it is child's play to agree about removing the hindrances compared with the problems of planned social action to enrich the quality of human life, whether through more satisfying personal relationships at every stage, or individual achievement, or delight in beauty and the arts.

Dr. Frankel does not regard the better life as simply a process by which specific ills are rectified. This seems to imply that sometimes negatives slide into positives, and that, hopefully, the drives to health, wholeness, and creativity in human beings, if given sufficient opportunity, assert themselves. We do not yet know under what circumstances or to what extent this is so. Dr. Frankel also repeatedly implies that conflict and change are alike both inevitable and desirable, but that there are also fundamental ideals or bounds within which a problem is defined. He specifies liberty and equality but wisely leaves each of us to fill in the rest for ourselves by calling it "et cetera." That "etc." is the real battlefield, but at least liberty and equality are circumscribing ideals which rule out authoritarianism as a convenient means or an inevitable consequence of a closer approximation between social theory and social practice. This makes the challenge of the task all the greater.

This is a fitting point at which to pause and take heart. The imbalance between different segments of the whole field of knowledge in the natural and social sciences, and between their application in the light of social theory, is all too apparent; so also is the gap between knowledge, motivation, and the rational use of the intellect and emotions. But, nonetheless, it is well to remember that until quite recently the better life meant a better life for the few; that liberty meant freedom from gross oppression, not a multi-sided economic, political, and religious freedom and social mobility; and that equality, whether of classes, sexes, or races was—and in some quarters still is—a pernicious heresy. Moreover, not only are the natural sciences quite recent on the scale of their present application, but also the social and behavioral sciences date only from the last century in a rudimentary scientific form, as distinct from a branch of philosophy or the stored wisdom and folly of human experience.

This, then, is the first century to witness the beginnings of large-scale and systematic attempts to apply, however fitfully, the principles of liberty, equality, and "etc." to human affairs, with the aid of scientific tools and new social inventions. For the first time, too, the earliest halting attempts are being made to implement these ideals for all classes, colors, creeds and both sexes—even children —not only within a nation, but also internationally. Admittedly, in this century of violent contrast, wars and ideological conflict have torn asunder the bonds of common humanity more effectively than efforts to strengthen them. But this has happened all through history and is less significant than the means we now possess to add new dimensions to liberty and equality.

For most of us, the application of theory to practice is a response to the groundswell of our day and nation and is undertaken in humble ways. It is nonetheless well that we should pause from time to time to reflect that our attitudes, aims, and values stem from one or another of the great social theories which have moved mankind, whether the four standard views so incisively reviewed by Dr. Frankel, or other philosophies, and that to know why we do what we do is as important as being able to do it.

COMMENTARY

WHITNEY M. YOUNG, JR.

Dr. Frankel's excellent paper does not lend itself to serious disagreement.

Having spent some eight years in academia, as a dean and professor, and some twelve years in the field of practice, I have for a long while been greatly concerned about something that Dr. Frankel touched upon: the apparent inability of social scientists to develop the same degree of compatibility between researchers and practitioners, or between theorists and actionists, as has been developed by the natural scientists. We still hear—all too often— the practitioner discredit the researcher by categorizing him as an ivory-tower quarterback who, while astute in describing and identifying the phenomena, is completely incapable of doing anything about the social disorganization. On the other hand, we have the extreme of the theorist and the researcher who point to the practitioner and say he is cooking by taste and playing by ear, and that he is totally incapable of developing a scientific approach to his program or to his action. This has disturbed me, because I think we all suffer from these kinds of morbid generalizations, and so I want to be sure to contribute anything I can to a happier marriage of the two.

I think that it's extremely difficult to be critical. Dr. Frankel in his paper is so studied in his objectivity and so completely clear in his approach, that it is difficult to determine what he advocates or what he criticizes in the four major approaches that he outlines— and this I say by way of admiration and not criticism. (I think that at worst he can accuse me of "nit-picking.") Having had his paper for a month, I've had opportunity to do some interpreting and to take this brilliant, theoretical exposition—this very elaborate dissertation—and bring it down to the language of some of us earthbound people so we might understand it better. Again, this is not criticism; it is admiration.

Dr. Frankel has presented four approaches to the old question as to whether man can apply moral judgments to social phenomena and to what extent. He has given us a sophisticated analysis of the perennial debate between idealism and determinism as it relates to social institutions. The idealist seeks first to define *what ought to be* the idea of the Good, while basically either ignoring *what is* or discounting the factors which prevent the perfect society from becoming a reality. For example, how can imperfect man build a perfect world? This view has the earmarks of the "to dream the impossible dream" approach. But it serves the need in social action in that it provides the passion, the idealistic motivation which the pure pragmatist lacks. I think immediately of people in the field of civil rights like Dr. Martin Luther King, and I think of people in international relations like Linus Pauling. Both groups are very necessary to our society if we are to give intelligent attention to the issues; both men possess this passion and the idealistic motivation in large measure.

Dr. Frankel's conservative view is clearly determinism. This view, I feel, probably relies too heavily on tradition. If man is deprived of tradition, he has little else on which to base his behavior because in ideas so complex, man cannot depend entirely on intellectual theory to guide his actions. To keep social action going other traditions should be used. All ideas have some tradition in them inasmuch as changes are made in response to their assessment and reassessment of the past and the present. The flaw, it seems to me, in the conservative view is that it gives many people an excuse for standing still or even regressing. This view assumes that all tradition is *ipso facto* good. This is where we run into practical trouble with the states-righter, who still thinks our country is safe and secure behind the "wall" of the Pacific and the Atlantic Oceans, and who feels that a man, if he's got any get up and go, need never be on relief or need never have any assistance. Citing tradition is the easy solution for many people. Even the Muslims cant that the problem of the Negro in the ghetto is one of an innately evil white man who is congenitally corrupt and morally bankrupt; the "traditional" answer to the problem is to get away from him or destroy him.

Dr. Frankel's third approach, historicism, appears to be closely related to determinism in the sense that it assumes that there are certain immutable laws of history which shape and govern social change, so that the free will of men, expressed individually or in groups, is minimized or discounted altogether. The individual should not try to interfere with this "plan of history," but should adjust himself to it and arrange to move along the direction that history appears to be taking. Social work, I think, has already gone through that unenlightened period and no longer suffers from this concept which makes it a necessity for man to adjust to his environment however evil and corrupt and harmful that environment might be.

Time solves nothing; men do. The simple ticking of the clock never brought about a single social reform. The danger in the simple historic approach is that it permits people to escape from involvement and responsibility. Karl Marx based his plan on the theory of the inevitable collapse of capitalism. To depend on the historic approach presupposes that historical events are logical, rational, and interrelated, which is a false assumption. History is not the result of predetermined series of facts or fate. Nothing is irredeemable until it is a fact. The important changes in the Negro problem, says Gunnar Myrdal, are not closely related to social trends in the narrow meaning of the term, but are changes in people's beliefs and customs. It seems to me that historicism ignores man's ability to make adjustments and accommodations whenever self-interest is threatened. Again, there are some in the Negro community (the Baldwins, the Le Roi Joneses) who talk about the decadence of the white society and how it will inevitably destroy itself by its own corruption. It would be very difficult for me to plan a program in the Urban League based upon the collapse of the white society. I tend to believe that white society is flexible and intelligent, so that it must make and will make necessary adjustments.

Dr. Frankel's fourth and final approach, "piecemeal social engineering," seems to be a higher synthesis which draws valid elements from the three earlier approaches and rejects those aspects which seem to be no longer valid in view of our increased knowledge of human individual and group behavior. The term "realism," it appears to me, would be more appropriate to describe this approach for it rejects the naïveté of the pure idealist without surrendering the right to pass moral judgments on social phenomena (as does the pure determinist or conservative). The phrase "piecemeal social engineering" appears to be deficient in that it implies much too narrow an area for social action. To say that reform will be undertaken only on those issues which, to quote Dr. Frankel, "do not arouse deep-seated moral disagreements" is to make consensus a necessary precedent to action, and to ignore the constructive role of conflict in the resolution of social issues. Conflict, power—and even coercion—are desirable and often very necessary tools in the achievement of constructive social change.

This is why I do not despair of progress in American race relations because of occasional violence, riots, and other confrontations. Where there is obviously a condition of inequity existing without any conflict, the victim is either completely resigned to his fate or so completely suppressed that he dare not protest. I do, however, deplore society's almost total preoccupation with the few instances of violent conflict while ignoring the many acts of progress and cooperation. And I have nothing but contempt and disgust for those who would penalize and judge the many for the acts of a few. I feel particularly strong about this right now since so many people have been telling me recently that we lost the civil rights bill and we are alienating a few of our good, dear friends because a handful of Negroes got involved in some riots and some excessive action. I think it's well to note at the end of another "long, hot summer," that 17,990,000 Negroes out of a potential 18,000,000 did *not* throw any rocks, did *not* throw any Molotov cocktails, did *not* riot, and *did nothing* but remain patient and restrained and hopeful that somehow the society would rise to a level of decency. For every one person who threw a rock this summer, over a thousand Negro boys were being sacrificed in Vietnam. It's good to remember this and to say, "We will support a civil rights bill and we will be your friends because those hundreds died," instead of, "We will do nothing because those dozens threw rocks." History will some-day, it seems to me, record the people who have been the truly violent, callous, immoral people in American society, and it will reserve its strongest indictment for neither the few of good will nor the few of ill will, but for the eighty to eighty-five per cent of the people who have no will.

May I also add that American Negro citizens today need no condescending or patronizing advice or counseling about restraint and patience whether that advice comes from very high places or very low places. We hold the copyright on patience and restraint. What we need are jobs, housing, training, opportunities, and allies who do not panic and run from the cause because a few well-publicized, desperate, and adventurous youngsters adopt a slogan called "Black Power."

A fundamental point which needs to be made here is that there is far more that man can do to eliminate suffering, iron out in-equalities, and achieve a more equitable distribution of the benefits of technology than has ever been done or has yet been generally realized. We have come so recently out of an era in which inequal-ities, poverty, and human deprivation were accepted as a matter of course and as an inevitable part of the human estate, that somehow I feel we still adopt this attitude. Idealists, moralists, and philoso-phers have always talked about utopia but have seldom, if ever, had the necessary resources or the vision to specify how they would implement their ideas. Today, at least in this nation, the resources are at hand and there is an increasing understanding of human behavior and the means by which society can open new doors of opportunity and give every man a chance to develop to his maximum potential.

Finally, I would offer the converse of Dr. Frankel's assertion that "some people inevitably pay for other people's added increments of welfare." For example, when an organization like the Urban League helps a Negro family to move from dependency to independent self-support, it has produced dividends which are enjoyed by everyone. In other words, the total community now derives the benefit of one more productive and self-supporting tax-paying family unit. The sooner we can see assistance and training of all types as investments rather than as sacrifices, the better off we will be.

Dr. Frankel seems to preface his thesis on the assumption that it is always the majority in society that determines the course for all, yet the American Negro in the current social revolution may have the higher moral theory and make the majority of society better as a result of initiating social action that was not anticipated or even intended by the majority in society. And again, I think history will show that the new attention given to education, new Federal aid to education, the poverty program, the rent-supplement bills, the demonstration cities legislation, and much of the social legislation we have gotten for all people in the society, has probably been triggered by the so-called Negro Revolution. The cost—in the sense of being forced to accept changes—is of no consequence; and, as a matter of fact, the changes can even prove beneficial and enjoyable once the initial shock is over, and people learn the beauty of diversity and the strength of a pluralistic society. Good examples are open-occupancy housing and the integrated foxholes of Vietnam.

The suggestion that "piecemeal social engineering" applies only to developed industrial societies appears to ignore the tremendous impact of community development efforts in under-developed nations around the world. The outlook of the target population need not be already sympathetic to the idea of social innovation to appreciate the value of a dam which will provide irrigation for crops or the value of innoculations which will reduce disease.

Dr. Frankel employed the term "racial prejudice" as a source of suffering which needs to be controlled. It would be more accurate to use the term "racial discrimination." The attitude is far less damaging than the act. For those who would assert that action flows from attitudes, it is relevant to point out that to an even greater degree, the attitude results from the pattern of action to which individuals and groups have been accustomed. Thus agencies and organizations, like the Urban League, which are change agents, are much more concerned with modifying behavior through enlightened policy decisions and constructive legislation, than with seeking changes in what President Eisenhower used to call "the hearts of men." In seeking change, thinkers as far apart as Karl Marx and William Graham Sumner are in agreement that institutional change results more quickly from changes in the economic area than in any other aspect of community life. Thus, in making necessary choices as to points of emphasis in seeking change, it is almost universally true: the top priority should go to economic development activities in poverty programs and related efforts. And remember, it is not a lack of education or a lack of economic resources or a lack of cultural appreciation that keeps Ralph Bunche, who has a Nobel Peace Prize, a Phi Beta Kappa Key, and a Ph.D., out of Cicero, Illinois, though Al Capone could and did live there—it is the color of his skin.

THE RESPONSE

CHARLES FRANKEL

I'm going to try not to take too much of the time of the distinguished discussants to discuss their remarks at length. I think, on the whole, there is very basic agreement among us.

I was particularly grateful to Dame Younghusband for her final remarks because I thought two of them in particular caught pretty much the essence of what I wanted to say. The first concerned liberty, equality, and *et cetera*. That each of us has to fill in the *et cetera* explains why trouble arises over ideas about which we apparently agree. And yet the trouble is worthwhile because (as explained by her second remark) it is really as important to know why we do things as to go ahead and do them.

The other remarks that were made by the discussants were

extremely helpful to me in pulling together what I was trying to say.

Mr. Young, I think, misunderstands me on some points. For example, he claims that I say "piecemeal social engineering" does not apply to developing societies and then he points out the great role of community organization. But, of course, I agree with him. I do find "piecemeal social engineering" at fault in relation to problems of the developing societies, because, in fact, it has neglected community organization. It has usually gone in and said, "Let's look at the market system," or "Let's look at chemical fertilizers," and so forth, and hasn't gotten into the sociological and anthropological study of the community texture.

I also agree with his remark, by the way, that what counts is not so much changing "the hearts of men" as changing their behavior. I would only add that when we change their behavior, after a while they begin to wonder what in the world they were so fearful of and their hearts change, too. The best way to change people's attitudes over an extended period of time is, through law and in other ways, to change the conditions under which people must operate. But he did ask me a really fundamental question—though he asked it kindly and as a kind of joke—in noting that my remarks left him wondering what in the world it was that I advocated. He said that I had taken a proper scholarly position but had left everyone a little frustrated. My old friend, Charlie Schottland, asked the same question. He said, "You took care of everybody and left us with no firm base on which to act; you left us, at best, with piecemeal social engineering." No, I think I left you with that, plus insights from the other points of view, plus, above all, a humanistic politics. I have felt very strongly in my own recent life, as you well understand, what it means to move from the level of theory to the level of practice. I do not regret the move at all. I've had a marvelous and exciting time; but it is, of course, quite a different life. I do not walk into government committee meetings with the thought that we must all first agree on ideology—or on spelling out the *et ceteras*—before we get together on some practical action. I think the basis for effective action in a diverse society is precisely to focus on problems that everyone will accept as problems and look for a resolution to a problem that everyone is likely to accept more or less. But I

don't agree that any acceptable solution is likely to make everybody happy.

The solutions we find may indeed contribute to the greater welfare
of the community as a whole but that doesn't make everybody happy
—there are still some buzzards who don't want to do what makes
everybody happy. There hasn't been a decision I've taken over the
last year that hasn't made somebody angry and, in fact, I wouldn't
have thought the decision was important unless it made somebody
angry because it wouldn't be changing anything of importance.
Whenever you change anything of importance, somebody objects,
although it may not be for a very real reason. Just the other day
someone working for me said, "Oh, we can't do that." I said, "Why
not?" "Because we've been doing it differently for twenty years."
Well, of course it's pain to change and however you do it somebody
is going to be opposed. But I do think, at the level of practice, that
it's important to try to keep questions of ultimate principle out
of the immediate context of action. However, you can convert this
virtue, which is (on the whole) a virtue of American democracy at
its best. American democracy at its worst is full of ideology. Listen
to Congressional debates, look at the civil rights issue, look at the
opposition to elementary moves in the civil rights area. The opposition is ideological; it happens to be the wrong ideology, but it is
ideological—and very often superstitious. Certainly, however, when
we work at our best, we do so by keeping arguments about ultimate
ends out of the picture. Yet even this great virtue can have a defect.

I suppose, as a man who has spent his life in philosophy, I can't
help being both impressed and depressed by the thousands of
faithful government servants who go to work every day, work hard,
and go home in the evening, and really haven't much idea why
they are doing what they are doing. And for that matter, I get
depressed at the political debates that take place because they con-
sist very largely in debates over unrealities. I often feel that if these
people would only, in the privacy of their own rooms, ask themselves
"What is it I want?" then at least there would be more intellect in
the activity.

I do think that in a society like the United States or any free
society there can be no agreement on any single set of fundamental
values. I would, myself, place such great stress on diversity as a

fundamental value that if this total agreement were possible, I would deplore it. I much prefer a society in which there is diversity over fundamental styles, over conceptions of the good life, and the like; what I hope does not happen is that we convert our success in pragmatic, political activity into a virtue that consumes everything else.

There ought to be in our schools of social work, there ought to be in our universities, there ought to be in our intellectual life, a much more explicit discussion and debate about what it is that we think a better society would be. There ought to be much more explicit effort to find out what the cost is of the things we take for granted, to find out what our values really are when we spell out what their conditions and consequences are and make the determination that, despite these conditions and consequences, we still want them.

There is, in any society, a necessity to choose; and there is, in most men, a desire to obfuscate or obscure the choice—a desire to make it look as though we can have both sides, as though we can have our cake and eat it too. If I had to say what was "original sin" in man, I'd say it was this: that man wants things, but doesn't want to pay the price for what it is he wants. He doesn't want to give up certain things; he wants everything. But man cannot have everything.

As one now in practical politics, I think I know as well as the next fellow that we can pour a little honey, but *entre nous*, as one now in the university scene, I can say—and feel sure you will agree—that pouring honey isn't the role of universities any more than it is the role of churches. A university ought to be a center of abstract thought, abstract criticism, and a center for discussion of the basic choices. When the academician goes out in the world, he doesn't have to carry everything he knows with him in the front of his mind; certainly he ought to avoid having it on the tip of his tongue. I don't want ideological debate. But he ought to have his own sense of what he'd like a society to be, at least consciously, in the back of his mind. And that leads, I think, to the real issue which we were debating here, and Mr. Young, Mr. Schottland, and Dame Younghusband have all helped me to see it. They may not agree, but this is the way I would see it.

Over the long course of history, societies have accepted certain explicit schemes of belief and value, "ideologies" if you will. Most societies have been dominated by some single scheme. Practically all these schemes have rested either on divine revelation or on some statement with which all rational men were expected to agree. As a result of the growth of science and democracy and liberalism, these ideologies have gradually been forced into retreat. In consequence, the classic functions of both theology and philosophy in the social field have disappeared. People have felt that somehow ideology, as such, was bad; that philosophy—the effort to clarify the grounds of belief, to find out what people want when they are most serious and self-examining—that philosophy, as such, is an illusory enterprise. We are, I think, in a kind of in-between position, perhaps, in the evolution of the human mind and its own conception of itself. There has been, I think, a positivistic excess to compensate for the old theological excess. The question in my mind is whether it is possible to have a philosophy which is experimental and scientific and which holds its values as provisional; which is hypothetical and subject to change; and which still does—for individuals and for social discourse and social debate—one of the jobs that classic philosophies did. Classic philosophies are among the causes of human hostilities and war. Ideological frenzy today is a great cause of war. But it does not seem to me to mean that the cure is to do without clarity or philosophy. If there is a condemnation to be made of American society a hundred years from now, I think one of the things people will say about us is that with all our affluence we never really seriously got down to business and asked what it was that our experiment in civilization was all about.

II

THE ESSAY

A Subversive Version of the Great Society

MICHAEL HARRINGTON
Author of *The Other America* and *The Accidental Century*

COMMENTARY

RICHARD A. CLOWARD
Professor of Social Work, Columbia University School of
Social Work

JOHN B. TURNER
Professor of Social Work, School of Applied Social
Sciences, Case Western Reserve University

ALTON A. LINFORD
Dean, School of Social Service Administration, University
of Chicago

THE RESPONSE

MICHAEL HARRINGTON

THE ESSAY

A Subversive Version of the Great Society

MICHAEL HARRINGTON

In the first half of the 1960's, important people proposed that the United States make a social revolution but without the inconvenience of changing any basic institutions.

The President declared "unconditional war" on poverty and the Congress obligingly proclaimed that it was the public policy "to eliminate the paradox of poverty in the midst of plenty." This goal and the abolition of racial injustice as well were "just the beginning," according to Lyndon Baines Johnson. The Chief Executive looked toward nothing less than a Great Society, "a place where men are more concerned with the quality of their goals than the quantity of their goods," where leisure would mean "a welcome change to build and reflect, not a feared cause of boredom and restlessness," where the city would serve "the desire for beauty and the hunger for community."

An excellent case can be made for dismissing all this talk as windy futurism.

For one thing, America has yet to fulfill the hopes of the last generation of reform. In 1944, for instance, Franklin Roosevelt advocated a genuine, legally guaranteed right to work; if the private sector failed to provide a man with a job, the public sector would be obliged to create a useful employment for him. But by the time a conservative Congress got through with this fine affirmation in the Employment Act of 1946, the President's binding promise of work had been downgraded to the status of a pious wish. There followed two decades in which intolerable rates of unemployment were chronic. In the late forties, Harry S Truman put forward a health-insurance plan which would cover every citizen. It then took twenty years of bitter struggle to gain such protection under Medicare for the 10 per cent of the population over 65 years of age.

Perhaps the final and most ironic disappointment is that in 1966 the nation had not yet constructed the number of low-cost housing units which Senator Robert Taft, the leading conservative of his time, had targeted for 1955.

So, if the realization of the old-fashioned reforms has been so half-hearted, there is good reason to suspect new utopias. Suspicion is particularly valid when President Johnson suggests that fundamental transitions in American life and values are to be achieved almost effortlessly. The corporations and the unions, the racial majority and the minorities, the religious believers and the atheists, the political machines and the reformers—all are supposed to unite in making a reasonable, conflict-less upheaval. And in a country where making money has traditionally been the most revered goal, suddenly transcendental, spiritual considerations are going to come first.

It is easy enough to make fun of the Great Society. And to do so is wrong. For the new rhetoric is an admission of how deeply troubled this land is, of how much remains to be done, and the task is in no way diminished if that rhetoric is inexcusably vague about how to solve the problems which it recognizes. It is an enormous gain that the leaders of the nation have admitted that they are confronted with a situation which requires nothing less than new principles. That is a crucial point of departure for the concerns of this colloquium—for social theory and social innovation. And the next step is to start talking about the actual, specific details of the transition to a humane future.

It is of the greatest significance that the government now freely admits that every big city in America is in a financial, racial, and social crisis. This situation does indeed touch the intimate intangibles of the qualities of our life as realistically as it affects the quantities of the Gross National Product. It makes old age lonelier, youth more rootless, the streets more chaotic.

Furthermore, it should be obvious that a program like the Demonstration Cities proposal fails utterly to deal with these realities. The President asked for $400 to $500 million a year over five or six years; Senators Kennedy and Ribicoff rightly implied that this was not enough; thereupon Mayor Lindsay noted that the city of New York alone could spend $50 billion to make the city livable. Then Senator Kennedy totaled up the various mayoral estimates and announced that they would total a trillion dollars over the next period. He apparently believed that this constituted a *reductio ad absurdum,* not realizing that projecting the sum over twenty years of escalating GNP, it would not be too much more than the 3 per cent of national product which Harry Truman asked for in 1947 in order to rebuild Europe. But there is no point in arguing the sums, for the Congress is clearly intent on disappointing Mayor Lindsay and Senators Kennedy and Ribicoff as well as President Johnson.

But instead of mocking the contrast between the Presidential rhetoric and the Congressional action, there is a more subversive strategy: that is to take the Great Society seriously.

A living precedent should explain the meaning of this tactic. In recent years the American Negro, after enduring some centuries of white inhumanity and hypocrisy, "outrageously demanded" that the society live up to its own pieties. Words about equality and justice, which for generations had been as empty as a ceremonial Fourth of July speech, suddenly became the programs and slogans of a militant mass movement. All of this was not accomplished, let it be emphasized, by conciliation and good will. The dynamic was conflict and the actual involvement of dedicated, literal-minded fighters who were willing to die for the idea of Freedom.

The Great Society is not going to be handed down from on high any more than the Negro will be graciously conceded his democratic rights by the white majority. To build "a place where men are more concerned with the quality of their goals than the quantity of their goods" is a most urgent imperative in the last third of the twentieth century, for if society is not made great, it will most likely become monstrous. This is the realistic element in the Presidential talk and it is an important point of departure. But to breathe life into the Johnsonian abstractions is going to take a radical restructuring of American values and practices, and that demands political struggle and conflict. There are powerful forces in this land which profit from and therefore promote the mediocre society; they are unalterably opposed to the best possibilities of the future.

In 1966, a sober government commission, composed of business-men, scholars, civil-rights leaders, and trade unionists, proposed that the United States take specific and concrete public action to place human considerations above mere money making. It is a measure of the depth of the present crisis that it drives practical men to visions.

The report, *Technology and the American Economy*, prepared by the National Commission on Technology, Automation and Economic Progress, asked that the "government explore the creation of a 'system of social accounts' which would indicate the social benefits and social costs of investments and services and thus reflect the true cost of a product. In such an approach, production and innovation would be measured, not simply in terms of its profitability to an individual or a corporation, but in relation to how it affects the society—of its profitability from the standpoint of the common good. There would be over-views of entire areas of social need, like housing and education, and analyses of the Gross National Product from the point of view of economic opportunity and social mobility." This information, the Commission said, would help us to calculate the "utilization of human resources in our society...."

This idea of social costs is one of the most radical suggestions to have been put forth by a responsible body in the recent history of the United States. The idea is not, of course, a new one, but the notion of putting the government behind it, of translating it from social science into politics, is a threat to some of our most cherished injustices.

Social accounting would inevitably attack the power of both the automobile and real estate industries. It would probably force the country to consider putting an effective end to both cities and states as its fundamental subdivisions. And it would most certainly promote bitter conflict between the partisans of the private interest and the defenders of the public good.

Another sober, moderate document—the 1966 Report of the Council of Economic Advisors—points unerringly, and perhaps unwittingly, at some of these extraordinary implications of social accounting. The Council itself generally represents the responsible, Keynesian center ground of American thinking. It is, of course, a proponent of government intervention into the economy. But then, with the exception of a few incurable ideologists, so is most of big business—as corporate support for tax cuts and the candidacy of Lyndon Johnson in 1964 demonstrated. Moreover, the Council rejects the radical thesis that problems like unemployment, poverty, and racism are, to a considerable degree, structured into the technology and that there must be fundamentally new mechanisms to deal with them. Instead, it believes that the crucial role for Washington is to make sure that there is enough effective consumer demand to buy what the private sector produces. These days, that is an orthodoxy which is as welcome on Wall Street as at Harvard.

And yet, for all this hard-headedness, the Council used nearly alarmist words to describe the somber plight of the American city. "Almost without exception," it said in the 1966 Report, "the central core cities, which are the heart of the metropolitan area, have experienced a gradual process of physical and economic deterioration. Partly as a result of people's desire for more space and home ownership, and made possible by the development of the automobile, central cities have been losing middle- and upper-income families to the suburbs. This movement accelerated when cities became caught in a vicious spiral of spreading slums, rising crime and worsening congestion. . . . This process created an almost impossible financial situation for many cities."

The Council then added a little detail. Many families have moved to the suburbs but their jobs have stayed behind in the metropolis, so there are vast hordes of commuters who come into the central city each day. At the same time, urban land values have been on the increase, and consequently tall, densely packed buildings have become the rule. As a result, the number of people who have to go to a particular point at approximately the same time increases tremendously and the transportation system is strained to the limits. By the end of the day, hundreds of thousands of people have experienced the social cost of congestion, traffic jams, frayed nerves.

As a description, all this is familiar enough. But then the Report turns toward that evaluation which is so essential to any system of social accounting (and to any society where men make the "quality of their goals" more important than the "quantity of their goods"). At this moment of truth, the Council becomes diplomatically vague and evasive. It describes how the builders do not have to bear the cost of the daily problems which their work causes and thus forces local governments to make large investments in transportation. Then comes a most delicate remark: "From the point of view of efficiency, these investments often should have been made in facilities for mass transit. Instead, *for many reasons,* they have been primarily in automobile expressways, which only increase the congestion at the center." (Emphasis added.)

It is no accident that the Council becomes so imprecise at the exact moment when it must assign responsibility for the urban crisis it has defined. Among the "many reasons" left unspecified is the decision to invest in expressways (and congestion) rather than in mass transit—a decision which bows to two lobbies, both of which are economically and politically potent: those of automobile and real estate industries. And if there is to be effective social accounting, the value judgments will thus inevitably come into conflict with those most autarchic American planning authorities, the big corporations.

The automobile is, of course, the beneficiary of enormous public subsidies which give it tax support in wreaking social havoc. Roads are among the few things which conservative Republican Congressmen are hellbent to socialize. The total cost of the Interstate system is currently estimated at $46.8 billion, and, as of June, 1965, the Federal aid and Federal highway projects approved or under construction were worth almost $14 billion. If such a sum were dispensed at the same time to deal with the misery of the people in the cities, there would probably be charges of Red Revolution.

But then, part of these funds are supplied by a "user" charge paid by car owners and truckers. Only these contributions don't begin to make the automobile pay its way. For in addition to the outright grants from Washington, the car imposes an enormous number of additional costs upon the society. Highway patrolmen, parking space, and traffic systems are obvious cases in point. And, for that matter, Charles Abrams has noted that the annual cost of the traffic jam—in terms of time and wages lost, extra fuel consumption, vehicle depreciation, etc.—is of the order of $5 billion.

Another social cost of the car intensifies the misery of the poor and reinforces racial discrimination. In the Watts area of Los Angeles, the White House Conference on Civil Rights reported, workers had to travel two hours, transfer to several bus lines, and pay half a dollar each way to commute to jobs or visit employment offices. "These transportation difficulties," a Conference report said, "discourage job seekers and impose unfair costs on workers least able to meet them."

In short, the care and feeding of the automobile often receives more vigorous government support than the care and feeding of people. Indeed, I have previously suggested that if Congress adopted the semantic procedure of referring to the poor as "cars" and to poverty as "wasted highway space," the legislators would enthusiastically vote to end "the other America" within a matter of a few years.

Yet the public has only the vaguest idea of how much its beloved cars really cost. There is considerable popular contempt for mass transit, but how much is this due to the fact that the subway has had to pay its own way while the automobile was freeloading? It could be that the people, after learning the true price of the car in terms of air pollution, poverty, racial discrimination, nervous disorders, and the destruction of beauty, would still opt for more disaster. But a national presentation of the social accounts for transit would much more likely lead to a new allocation of resources —and the car might even be taken off the dole.

All of this leads one to suspect that the automobile industry would be flatly opposed to such an honest and democratic undertaking. In the spring of 1966, the car makers dismissed analyses of the lack of safety in their product and, inadvertently it was said, attempted to assemble a blackmailer's dossier on their chief critic. It was only when it became clear that there was a political *force majeure* in favor of reform that the corporate giants began to seek a compromise. This did not happen because Detroit is inhabited by a race of unique rich demons. It represents the instinctive response of the profit maker faced with social regulation. The drug industry fought in 1962 against effective public controls over its power of life and death; the steel industry allowed President Kennedy to persuade the union to observe wage guidelines while it was preparing to break the price guidelines; and so on. The automobile industry, then, has a vested interest in our present urban crisis.

So does real estate. The White House Civil Rights Conference got a large portion of this truth when it reported that "Federal housing policy until recently was geared almost exclusively to a market of middle class families who desired to live in the suburbs. This was, and *remains*, a market from which Negroes and the poor are virtually excluded." In short, there has been enormous public financial support to the well-off and practically nothing for the poor. And the private interests of real estate developers have thus been promoted by tax funds and with stunning social effect.

At this point there is only space enough to note a few of the ways in which this reactionary subsidy was implemented. The Federal government generously provided much of the credit for suburbia (through the FHA, VA, FNMA, and other agencies)—at the same time as it was supposed to be enticing the middle class back into the central city through urban renewal. (There were cases, like the Title One scandal, in which speculators simply robbed the public.) More often, the real estate interests stamped the public programs with their private purposes in the full, legal light of day. As Professor James Q. Wilson of Harvard describes it, urban renewal at the local level was used "in some places to get Negroes out of white neighborhoods, in others to bring middle-class people closer to downtown department stores, in still other places to build dramatic civic monuments, and in a few places to rehabilitate declining neighborhoods and add to the supply of moderately priced housing."

Tax policy in this area was calculated to aid the better-off. In 1962, the estimated value of the tax deduction on mortgage payments was equal to about double the sum spent on public housing (a ratio of roughly $1.5 billion to $835 million). The poor got a cheap, inadequate, but highly visible subsidy; the self-reliant and virtuous middle class received a much more munificent, but socially invisible handout.

If there were social cost accounting, however, and the public moneys were actually used to redeem the official pledges about ending poverty and building a Great Society, it would mean the reversal of many of these postwar policies. Public housing would no longer be a matter of piling poor people on top of each other in segregated high-rise projects. The White House Conference on Civil Rights made a "conservative" estimate that the country needs

2 million new housing units a year instead of the 1.4 million now being built, and said that "at least half, preferably more" of the new units should be made available to low- and moderate-income families. The Conference also computed the cost of putting the poor in the private housing market through subsidies: to get all of the families with incomes under $3,000 into decent housing would take $10 billion.

The current Civil Rights struggle to open up habitable and integrated neighborhoods for the Negro has aroused some of the ugliest emotions in white America. And yet, if the nation were to change its present realty priorities of aiding the middle class while ignoring the poor—black and white—this conflict could be positively resolved. If Federal resources in the housing area were directed to fulfilling social needs rather than, as has been the case, promoting private profit, the slums and poverty could be abolished within ten years. And if there were decent housing for *all*, the economic and sociological basis of the present passions would be transformed. Moreover, integration could be advanced in the process. It is clear that there must be a planned extension of existing cities and the creation of "new towns" if American life is going to be tolerable, much less great, in the next generation. In the process, Washington could "discriminate" in favor of justice and equality by directing its subsidies to those blacks and whites, both middle-class and poor, who want to live together. This would be a considerable improvement over our recent patterns of aid to the white middle class.

Such an approach would outrage those who have prospered so much from our current injustices. This is why I suspect that a goodly portion of the real estate lobby would join the automobile industry in opposing sanity for our cities.

It is, of course, possible to argue that the changes in public policy involved in all this are too sweeping, the sums so astronomical, that such reform is out of the question. However, this argument also means a rejection of any pretense of building a Great Society; it supports a continuation of the present system of antisocial allocations: massive financing for the cars, roads, and housing of the suburban middle class; a further rotting of the central cities; an intensification of poverty and racial discrimination; pollution, congestion, ugliness; and so on down the list of the effective national priorities of America today. But if, as the National Commission on Technology, Automation and Economic Progress urges, a system of social accounting were adopted, it would then be possible to have rational debate—and even just laws. And that, the automobile and the real estate industries notwithstanding, is the *sine qua non* of a Great Society.

There should be a Council for the Great Society as part of the Executive branch. It should be charged by law with the preparation of an annual social accounting, a report on the quality of life in the United States and what can be done to improve it.

In making this suggestion, there is no implication that social accounting is a simple matter. There has been sharp, even acrimonious debate over the statistics and quantities which are the province of the Council of Economic Advisors. When human values and needs are at stake as well as the tangibles of a GNP, there is bound to be even more disagreement. There are, to take but a single instance, responsible and independent scholars who are much more optimistic about the automobile than I am. But even admitting all the difficulties, the arguments have to be taken out of the academies and made public.

One of the most effective single results of the Employment Act of 1946 has been that Washington has been obliged to become an economic educator. When the reports of the Council of Economic Advisors began, all the practical politicians had to pay their obeisance to myths about the balanced budget and to metaphors which compared a dynamic national economy to a prudent middle-class household. But now, some of the revolutionary concepts of a generation ago—the idea, for instance, that the government should measure the Gross National Product—have become commonplace and a kind of Keynesianism is the new orthodoxy. The sociologists —and the social critics, the visionaries—should now be given their chance to speak to this vast public audience.

Even if there were excellent social accounts and all the corporate obstacles to the common good were overcome, there is still another *status quo* with which we must deal. I refer to the Balkanized political map of the United States, which has more to do with the accidents of our history and the characteristic indifference of the

American people to its social responsibilities than it has to do with the needs of the nation.

The economy, the housing market, the transportation problems of an urban complex constitute a unity; the political jurisdictions in the same area are in fragments. Yet it is of the very essence of that "systems approach" which has succeeded so admirably for big business and the Department of Defense, that these issues be dealt with in their entirety, as part of a total system. In the course of the flight to the suburbs, the middle class feudalized the metropolitan areas. It liked to have the economic and cultural advantages of the big cities, but at the same time to live in pleasant little single-class baronies which allowed it to shun all the concomitant duties. Thus, as the government has now admitted, getting effective economic and social action on civil rights is going to require area-wide planning and action. (This was one of the conclusions of the White House Conference on Civil Rights.)

In 1966, the United States Conference of Mayors saw this approach as a practical necessity. The mayors urged the Federal government to withhold grants for community facilities, such as water and sewer systems, unless the recipient would agree to provide a "reasonable share" of low-income housing in the area. This was a reference to the suburban practice of enthusiastically taking Federal grants and devoting them to the exclusive use of the suburb's middle-class constituents. The mayors, arguing along similar lines, also demanded that Federal aid to education be made contingent upon an agreement by local authorities to accept pupils from poor districts, and to have government agencies promote the building of low-cost housing in *all* sections of the metropolitan area.

For years now, the United States government has recognized the justice of the mayors' point when it is applied to Europe or Latin America (Washington has been an international champion of regional integration and planning from the Marshall Plan to the Alliance for Progress). When, however, a similar need becomes desperately apparent within the United States, the policy is not so forthright. There have been some half-hearted attempts to tie some Federal funds to regional planning but, as the Mayors' Conference demonstrated, the suburbs still manage to direct most of the Federal funds into the construction of private Shangri-Las and to divert them from the urban crisis. There are some suburbanites—sincere religious people, contributors to Southern civil rights organizations, and so on—who may well conscientiously agree to surrender their selfish prerogatives. For the rest, tough Federal action will be required, like refusing to bankroll enclaves of middle-class irresponsibility.

There is a conservative myth in all of this which must be disposed of, for once and for all: The Federal government, it is said, is distant, impersonal, and bureaucratic; the "grass roots" are supposedly at local government where democracy is "pure," personal and vibrant. But in point of fact, the poor, the racial minorities, the organized workers—the majority of the American people—have found that Washington, D.C., is usually closer to their needs than their own city hall. It was, for instance, at the hallowed grass-roots level that urban renewal was so often made no more than an instrumentality of real estate profit. Indeed, it was precisely the power and domination of local conservatism which was a major element in driving reform away from the immediate community and toward Washington. Now, the blind selfishness of the suburbs is going to force a further increase in the Federal power with the result that the middle class is going to have to be drafted back into the American people. Unless, that is, there is an understanding that regional planning and investment is in the interest of the society as a whole.

But here, as in every other area of taking the Great Society seriously, one must expect conflict and political battles. For the central city dwellers might find it difficult to reason together with those suburbanites who have profited so much from the misery of the metropolis.

But then, governmental subsidies for the support of the commuter's car and local political irresponsibility are only part of a larger problem. As Washington has taken an increasingly activist role in the the national life, Federal policies have regularly favored the rich and discriminated against the poor and thus promoted the inequality of income distribution in the name of the common good.

A Great Society cannot tolerate such an official injustice. It would therefore move to reinstate one of the oldest and most "American" of the national ideals: Equality.

For it is one of the paradoxes of the sixties that there has been a significant rise in social consciousness but, with one exception, no heightened sense of egalitarianism. The only move for change with a genuine base in masses of people was the Negro struggle for civil rights. Here, the hundreds of thousands in the militant movement did not simply ask for "enough"; they demanded "more"— justice, the right of the Negro to be equal in every social and economic aspect of life. But the war on poverty, and the rest of the social programs of the sixties, had no such egalitarian dynamic.

The current rediscovery of the problems of the American underclass is not, by far and large, the product of a popular explosion like industrial unionism or some of the New Deal legislation in the thirties, or the Civil Rights Acts of 1964 and 1965. It began at the top of the society among concerned members of the intelligentsia; it occurred when the Cold War slackened and social criticism became less suspect; and it contained more than a little of that middle-class conscience which John F. Kennedy succeeded in evoking. After the riots in the ghettos of 1964, 1965, and 1966, these new antipoverty programs were also motivated by fear. When, for instance, Mr. Henry Ford came out in support of antipoverty efforts in 1966, he did so out of the explicit worry that if these miseries were not attended to, they might menace the *status quo*.

This *un-*, and even *anti-*, egalitarian trend toward social change is a typical prodigy of affluence. In the old days of, say, a generation ago, the demand for "enough" was simultaneously a demand for a more just sharing of the national income. The resources of the society were limited, and feeding and clothing and housing everybody decently required that income be redistributed from top to bottom. But with the unprecedented national products of the sixties, the political arithmetic of scarcity no longer held. There were, to be sure, limits on what could be done. And yet, the annual increments in production were so enormous that the well-off could finance new minimums for the poor and maintain the unjust structure of income distribution at the same time.

Perhaps the most simple illustration of this point can be made in terms of an oft-cited, and sometimes misleading, statistic. By spending about $13 billion in direct grants it would be possible to bring every American family over the poverty "line." (The feat would be, to a considerable degree, a statistical illusion, since enormous deficiencies in *social* consumption of housing, schools, health, clear air, etc., would remain even if the private incomes of the poor were all over the "line"—but that is another argument which is not relevant here.) Taking this estimate with the necessary care and qualifications, it is still significant that a statistical victory over poverty could be accomplished so cheaply. For $13 billion is not a terribly large sum in a GNP of over $700 billion.

In 1966 alone, something more than $13 billion was invested in the tragic war in Vietnam without straining the economy too much —and it certainly did not require that the rich receive less. In fact, the Vietnam war tended to redistribute income upwards to the wealthy. So it is now possible to conserve the injustice of our income structure and fight a war in Vietnam, or against poverty, at the same time.

Therefore it is necessary to inquire of an America which has only recently, and voluntarily, reacknowledged its obligations toward the poor, whether it still cares for its old ideal of Equality. The issue is not whether the nation should adopt an egalitarian utopia as a practical goal, but the real question is: Are we ready to take any steps, however tentative, toward a more just distribution of wealth?

For despite much journalistic and scholarly talk of recent social "revolutions," the American system of inequality has demonstrated a depressing vitality during the last two decades. In 1947, the poorest 20 per cent of the population received 5 per cent of the income, and it held that same 5 per cent in 1964 (all figures are taken from the September, 1965, Current Population Report of the Department of Commerce). The second lowest fifth got 12 per cent in 1947 and 12 per cent in 1964. In short, 40 per cent of the American people were held to a 17 per cent share of the income throughout this entire postwar period. *And the 5 per cent of the richest people received approximately as much as those 40 per cent at the bottom.* These figures understate the outrage since they are taken from tax returns where the highest income recipients hire expensive lawyers and accountants in order to conceal as much of their wealth as possible while the rest of the nation pays as it goes.

Now these terrible imbalances did not just happen. For one of the most powerful forces reinforcing these inequities was the United States government.

I do not suggest that there is, or has been, an anti-egalitarian conspiracy in Washington. It is simply that, *in the absence of strong and conscious countermeasures,* Federal action to guarantee the economic well-being of all will help the rich most and the poor least and thus strengthen the nation's pattern of inequality. This is an economy which is dominated by corporations and assigns its rewards unequally. If the government decides to stimulate this structure by providing incentives from the top down, then the accomplishment of the common good will inevitably discriminate in favor of the well-off and against the impoverished and even the middle class.

For instance, the tax cuts of 1962–65 were theoretically made impartially or, better yet, with higher percentages for the poor than for everyone else. But since those at the bottom have so little and those at the top so much—since the wealthiest 5 per cent have at least as much as the poorest 40 per cent—the actual cash savings were distributed overwhelmingly in favor of the rich. Thus, even on the level of a personal income tax reduction, federal policy resulted in a windfall for the wealthy. However, there was largesse for the corporations too, and this had nothing to do with the other Americans or even the middle class (the latter receive most of their income from salaries and fees, not from dividends or capital gains). As Theodore Sorenson noted in his biography of John F. Kennedy, the 1962 investment tax credit and new depreciation schedule were worth about $2.5 billion—the equivalent of an 11 per cent tax cut for activities which mainly benefit big stockholders, executives, and other unneedy types.

In addition, there were many, many other Federal benefits for the best-off Americans. Approximately 2 to 3 per cent of the GNP is devoted by Washington to research and development (mainly for defense and space), and this is contracted out to private firms which not only have a riskless profit in serving the common good but also acquire subsidized know-how. Thus the communications satellite technology was handed over to private interests free of charge—after private interests had made use of public money and personal profit in developing it. More recently, the *Wall Street Journal* has reported that the corporate sector looks upon anti-poverty projects as "blue chip," in part because they are an entree into the burgeoning "knowledge industry." Never has do-gooding been so handsomely rewarded than since big business got involved.

Many of these trends became most visible in the crisis of the "guidelines" policy of the Johnson Administration in 1966. For the 1962 investment tax credit had powered a gigantic capital goods boom; the other reductions in corporate taxes had been a tremendous incentive to the top; the income tax cut had put much more money in the pockets of the rich than in those of the poor; and so on. Thus, as prices went up, the percentage allocated to labor costs remained stable even though wages increased (between 1960 and 1965) by 33 per cent and, in the same period, after-tax corporate profits climbed by 67 per cent. In short, the Federal government had overpaid the businessman for being a good economic citizen and thus reinforced the income inequality of American society by the injudicious use of taxpayers' funds.

In short, if Washington intervenes in the economy and makes it more efficient, it will "impartially" favor those groups most powerfully organized to seize the incentives toward, and the fruits of, the new efficiency—unless there are active policies to combat this anti-egalitarian effect.

The single most important technique for increasing the GNP *and* taking some first steps toward equality *and* facing up to the critical problems which provoked the talk of the Great Society in the first place, is direct public investment in the areas of social consumption: housing for the poor, hospitals, schools, transportation systems, and the like. The entire society suffers from the deficiencies in these areas, but the poor suffer most of all, the workers next, the middle class next and the rich, the least, Therefore, in channeling funds into these areas, the common good would be served but the power of the government would be weighted on the side of those least able to take care of themselves, and not the other way around. If the Kennedy-Johnson tax cuts were taken as a percentage of the GNP and projected over twenty years, they would be in the neighborhood of that $1 trillion figure which Senator Kennedy found so fantastic. Why not invest this sum in social needs as democratically determined rather than leaving the decision of how to spend it up to individual and corporate consumers, and to rich individuals and corporations at that.

A second technique for introducing some egalitarianism into the society centers on tax policy. Historically, there has been a very serious political obstacle toward reform in this direction. The tax laws are so complicated, tricky, and inaccessible to the average man—and congressman—that the discussion is usually carried on by experts and special pleaders in their own labyrinthian way. The public has thus been excluded and even those concerned with positive change have been defeated.

Here is a situation where a Council for the Great Society would be of inestimable value. For the technicalities of the tax law are the means of assigning major social priorities: in favor of business through an investment tax credit; promoting marriage, and perhaps penalizing bachelorhood, through joint returns and deductions for children; aiding the middle-class home builder through mortgage write-offs and thus indirectly discriminating against the impoverished renter; and so on. A system of social accounting should spell out the major incentives and subsidies contained in the tax system and do so in *American English*. A nation which has been brought to an understanding of the relatively sophisticated point that Federal deficits can make money should be able to learn the social realities behind the tax system. Then it may well be possible to have fruitful debate—and reform.

But here again, in this area of attacking inequality, all will not be consensus and harmony. For the richest individuals and corporations have benefited enormously from these Federal policies which have kept the poor and everybody else in their (relative) place. For instance, Roger M. Blough, of U.S. Steel, told the National Industrial Conference Board in 1966 that the way to fight inflation was not through suspending the 7 per cent credit for business, i.e., not through Mr. Blough's surrendering some of the privileges which have brought the corporations excessive taxes, but through holding back on minimum wage and government welfare spending, i.e., for those least able to pay to shoulder the cost.

Thus, if there is to be any move toward equality in American society—and a more *just* distribution of the goods of the economy would obviously be the concern of a goal- and value-oriented Great Society—it will meet with determined political opposition. And in this undertaking, as in any drive for social cost accounting, *there will have to be determined and democratic conflict* in order to create new institutions as a response to unprecedented conditions.

These various ideas about taking the Great Society seriously point toward an ultimate conclusion which is more radical than any single proposal, at least to American ears. The profit motive can no longer be regarded as the keystone of economics and the test of patriotism. Putting it this way might seem unnecessarily candid. If, after all, reforms can be achieved in practice, why bother about first principles? Paradoxically, one reason for doing so is that plain talk on this issue might well make a Great Society more of a political possibility. For it speaks to the best, the most intelligent of the American youth today, the vanguard of a generation which is unprecedentedly large and has enormous potential for American politics.

In a very real sense, a growing number of young people have been following a system of personal social accounting in recent years. They have been allocating their lives on a basis of perceived need rather than of a hope for profit. More often than not, they have rebelled precisely because they have discovered that our professed ideals are so much cant. They will only listen to honest, straightforward talk, and that is why a frank avowal of the most radical deduction from the Great Society premise is an act of politics as well as of morality. It must be bluntly acknowledged that, if the high-flown talk about the Great Society is more than campaign oratory, then the nation's most beloved and anachronistic vulgarity —the faith in the primacy of private profit—must go.

Indeed, it should be quite obvious by now that if America is to be a place "where men are more concerned with the quality of their goals than with the quantity of their goods," it cannot honor greed as the inspiration of the individual and the supreme guide of the economy. Social accounting, investments in housing and transit on the basis of need, rational regional and national planning, are all encroachments upon the sovereignty of profit in the name of human need. In short, the Johnsonian rhetoric cannot be redeemed by simply making money.

Yet the mythology of profit still officially obsesses the nation—it is, for instance, wantonly taught to innocent school children. An almost pathetic illustration of this devotion to the old-fashioned untruths has been provided by the emergence of modified market principles ("Libermanism") in Russia and East Europe. The President was enormously cheered that "profits are coming to be understood as a better measure of productivity—and personal incentive as a better spur to effective action on behalf of the national economy." Neither Mr. Johnson, nor the editorialists who shared his jubilation, seemed to care that their hallowed free enterprise methods were being used by totalitarian bureaucracies in order to make controlled economies more efficient.

But then, perhaps the most authoritative testimonial on the possibilities of being done with the profit motive comes from a successful businessman, brilliant stock speculator—and a theorist who helped to save capitalism from itself. I speak, of course, of John Maynard Keynes.

In 1925 Keynes wrote, "... the moral problem of our age is concerned with the love of money, with the habitual appeal to the money motive in nine-tenths of the activities of life, with the universal striking after individual security as the prime object of endeavor, with the social approbation of money as the measure of constructive success, and with the social appeal to the hoarding instinct as the foundation of the necessary provision for the family and for the future." This statement anticipates the attitudes of many of the young American rebels of today. How it came from the pen of such a brilliant theoretical and practical entrepreneur is a fascinating moment in intellectual history. It is also quite relevant to the antiprofit implications of the Great Society.

Two years after this attack on the love of money, Keynes published a sophisticated and paradoxical distinction. There were two separate issues, he said; one concerned the efficiency of capitalism, the other the desirability of the system. "For my part," Keynes wrote, "I think that capitalism, wisely managed, can probably be made more efficient for obtaining economic ends than any alternative system yet in sight; but that in itself it is in many ways extremely objectionable." Eventually, Keynes believed, the economy would become so productive (he even imagined a zero rate of interest for capital) that society would no longer need to be immoral in order to be efficient. At that point, "The love of money—as distinguished from the love of money as a means to the enjoyments and realities of life—will be recognized for what it is, a somewhat disgusting morbidity, one of those semi-criminal, semi-pathological propensities which one hands over with a shudder to the specialists in mental disease."

This distinction between money as means and money as ends is crucial if the issues are not to be muddled. For the immediate future, and even in the visionary middle distance, almost everyone is going to devote himself to raising his standard of living and even pursuing luxuries. One accepts a modicum of self-interest and anti-neighborliness at this point in history. But it is another question as to whether these aspects of personality should be taken as the dominant principle of secular life in society. That, in essence, is the argument of the profit motive and it is, as Keynes described it, a "somewhat disgusting morbidity."

It is, however, a quite vital morbidity in the United States. How utterly fetishistic the pursuit of money can become was documented in the hearings of the Senate Subcommittee on Anti-Trust and Monopoly in 1964 and 1965. These investigations concentrated considerable attention on the "conglomerate enterprise." As one witness, Dr. Walter Adams, defined the phenomenon, it is "typically an aggregation of functionally unrelated or incoherent enterprises" under one firm. Textron, probably the largest American conglomerate, is thus an amalgam of 27 separate divisions and 113 plants, making helicopters, chicken feed, chain saws, mailboxes, portable space heaters, optical machinery, and radar antennae, to mention only a few items.

The function of such a structure has nothing to do with making things, much less quality goods. There can hardly be any central concern with workmanship when the corporation is indifferent as to whether it is making helicopters or chicken feed, optical machinery, or mailboxes. This is simply a way of making money as money and presumably Textron would make hydrogen bombs if the price were right. Once upon a time there was a savage ethical theory to justify such conduct. It was said that profiteering—outwitting one's fellow man, getting a special advantage, buying cheap and selling dear—was necessary in order to evoke the extremes of entrepreneurial ingenuity and dedication. Those were the heroic, dog-eat-dog days of the business civilization. Whether this morality was really ever needed, it certainly no longer holds. Research and development are government supported and largely carried out by scientific pieceworkers; corporations are more and more "rational," bureaucratic, private civil services rather than robber baronies. We are at that point foreseen by Keynes where the love of money need not be acknowledged as the arbiter of society's destiny.

The very best of the American young have intuited the Keynesian rejection of the money-making morbidity. They do not want to live their lives for Textron.

In 1964, the *Wall Street Journal* reported that 14 per cent of Harvard's senior class entered business—as opposed to 39 per cent in 1960. In 1966, the Harris Poll surveyed college seniors for *Newsweek* and found that this trend was deepening. Only 12 per cent of the sample were looking forward to business careers—and twice as many wanted to be teachers. Harris also reported that the acceptance of business as an institution in American society declined as education increased—that those with the most advantages were also the most alienated from the ruling economic ideology.

There was a humorous documentation of this pattern in an article by Roger Rapoport in a June, 1966, issue of the *Wall Street Journal.* A student who graduated with "the highest honors" at Michigan State University picketed his own commencement because of the presence of Vice President Humphrey, a supporter of the Administration's policy in Vietnam. This event, Rapoport said, was not an isolated occurrence. Michigan State has gone out to recruit genius as it once assembled football teams. As a result of an activist approach and generous scholarships, the University managed to attract 560 National Merit Scholars to East Lansing (Harvard, with the second highest Merit Scholar total, had 425).

But it turned out that it was precisely this intellectual elite which provided much of the impetus for campus dissidence and protest. The Merit Scholars were involved in publishing a newspaper critical of the University administration, attacking self-service laundry prices, and helping to document their own University's relations with the CIA in Vietnam. As Rapoport concluded, "The ironic situation in East Lansing points up a dilemma confronting a growing number of *quality-minded* universities these days." (Emphasis added.)

The Michigan State experience had, of course, been presaged at Berkeley where the student militants of the Free Speech Movement in 1965 were also from among the very best of the students. Indeed, one can speak of a deep current of antimaterialism and antibureaucracy among the most educated youth of the sixties. The brightest children of the affluent society have volunteered for dangerous civil rights projects in the South, for community organizing in the slums of the cities, for the Peace Corps, and for VISTA.

It could be that all this is only a phase. I think not. John F. Kennedy was among the first to understand that the youth of the sixties were much more readily moved by an appeal to sacrifice for the common good rather than by a scramble for private gain. In the vicious, competitive capitalist economy of the nineteenth century, it was at least possible to idealize a social Darwinist ethic. In the conglomerate enterprise of the mid-twentieth century, that is becoming infinitely more difficult. One can thus hardly suggest to a reflective, talented college senior that the point of all his training is to serve the interests of Textron.

Perhaps there is a new *Buddenbrooks* pattern emerging in the United States. In Mann's original chronology, the tough-minded merchants of the first generation were succeeded by ambiguous sons and ineffective, aesthetic grandchildren. In this country, it may well be that a more hopeful trend is developing as the educated grandchildren of immigrants become increasingly idealistic. If this is the case, then facing up to the fact that a Great Society cannot be built on a profit motive is an act of politics. Such clarity will have a profound appeal to the best of the young.

There must be specific and concrete proposals to show that quality really is being made sovereign over quantity. Perhaps the easiest proposal to adopt in this area was one made by Kingman Brewster, the president of Yale, in his inaugural address: Brewster said that social service should be given the same status as is now accorded to military training in our schools. The student who is preparing to be an officer receives various allowances for school and for summer training. The youth who wants to be a civil rights organizer or a Peace Corpsman, or to volunteer for any similar, useful activity, should have at least as much support.

In other words, it is not enough to sermonize the young that they should favor the Great Society. There should be new institutions to help those who want to build a new and exciting nation. The patriotism of life should be worth at least as much to America as the patriotism of death.

In conclusion, there is an unprecedented risk in talking utopian ideas today: for they have become possible and there is even a youthful political constituency which seems bent on taking them seriously.

This does not mean, as the rhetoric of the Great Society so often suggests, that some gigantic consensus is going to effortlessly revolutionize the United States without changing any basic institutions or old habits of thought. The society, economy, and political structure are magnificently organized in order to favor quantity over quality, to merchandise leisure like any other commodity, and to make the city a haven for ugliness and anomie rather than a servant of "the desire for beauty and the hunger for community."

Yet even though much of the speechmaking has been facile, it is significant and hopeful that pragmatic political leaders are being driven, by the radical character of the national plight, into visionary themes. So the President, and other very important people, have posed, perhaps unwittingly, a marvelous and subversive notion: the Great Society. It will require innovation, conflict, and institutional change, for it must inevitably challenge economic and political vested interests. I therefore propose this radical strategy—that we take the rhetoric of the President with utmost seriousness, that we redeem some of those phrases in the same militant way that Negroes have been redeeming the Declaration of Independence and the Emancipation Proclamation.

COMMENTARY

RICHARD A. CLOWARD

Let me say, first, that I share most of Mr. Harrington's perspectives on the major social problems in America to which he points.

He speaks eloquently and passionately in the cause of social justice.

Because I subscribe to so many of his specific criticisms of American life, I am especially saddened to find that I differ with Mr. Harrington's prescriptions for action to overcome them. I think, in fact, that the course he advocates would worsen the problems he so urgently wishes to solve.

Two major points emerge from his paper: first, that it would be useful to adopt programs of social accounting and planning; and second, that these techniques would enable us to rekindle our historic concern for equality. The latter problem is central to all of political history, but the prescriptions for action are modern and technical. I think we have already had enough experience with modern and technical approaches to know that they do not solve political problems. Indeed, techniques of social accounting and planning have already contributed to the entrenchment, if not to the enlargement, of the very inequalities against which Mr. Harrington speaks so forcefully.

Let me try to illustrate this point by drawing from my own field of social welfare. I was especially struck by Mr. Harrington's observation that America, by means of its fantastic affluence, is capable of abolishing poverty without threatening established inequalities in the distribution of income; and furthermore, it may very well do exactly that in the next decade through a guaranteed annual income financed from tax surpluses. The same point—that social arrangements can be humanized without in the least diminishing social injustice—can be made about many proposed reforms in social welfare.

One example that comes to mind is the many reforms proposed and effected in American agencies of criminal justice as they impinge on children. A host of reforms have been instituted which are intended to humanize the policies and practices of police and correctional agencies by substituting rehabilitation for punishment. Yet the reforms accept the fundamental inequities—especially along class and racial lines—which have always characterized law-enforcement and correctional practice at every stage. There is little evidence of reform in the decision to arrest, to charge, to prosecute, to place guilt, and to sentence. Indeed, most reforms hardly seem to recognize the existence of such injustices. These reforms, in short, seek to humanize systems without acknowledging, much less challenging, the fundamental inequalities upon which those systems are based. The same children who have always escaped the police system still escape it; those who have always been the system's victims continue to be its victims. To say that these systems are better because they are more benign is to miss the point.

This leads to another point, which would seem to be self-evident: the techniques we call "social accounting" and "social planning" have no inherent political volition. They may be rational, but I am certainly not prepared to identify the rationality of the technician with the common good. The fact is that these tools reflect the political interests of those who control the activities of the technician, and the vested political interests make decisions based on the resulting data. It is these interests which dictate the definition of the common good. Mr. Harrington seems to suggest otherwise when he states, "social accounting would inevitably attack the power and position of established and exploitative groups—such as the automobile and real estate industries." Perhaps this would be so if Mr. Harrington were in charge of the job and if he were given free rein, but those eventualities do not seem very likely. He suggests, further, that if we have social accounts, we will have social conflict. But why? I would have thought that the whole horrible panorama of American social problems, many of them created by government itself, would suggest the reverse proposition—that precisely because there are deep political interests at stake, there will be no social accounts that threaten these interests.[1]

Consider Mr. Harrington's description of the transportation problem confronting Watts. Certainly Watts has been ignored. Certainly it has been victimized by the automobile. But if a social accounting were made of the impact of highway development in Los Angeles, it seems unlikely that Watts would figure significantly in the analysis or conclusions. Very few Americans care much about Watts; very many care a great deal about their suburban homes and cars—and that is the central political reality. The related reality

[1] For a general discussion of the way in which professional bureaucracies serve to reduce conflict and to contain the poor, see Richard A. Cloward and Frances Fox Piven, "The Professional Bureaucracies: Benefit Systems as Influence Systems," in *The Role of Government in Social Change*, ed. Murray Silberman (New York: Columbia University School of Social Work, 1966).

is that technicians produce inevitably that which does reflect what most people care about, not what they do not care about or are antagonistic to. Even if a "rational" decision had been made to abandon highway development in favor of another mode of transportation, Watts would have been ignored. Suburban rapid transit rather than central city mass transit would probably have been elected, for historically, the accounters and planners have been responsive chiefly to the great and powerful suburban masses seeking a way to get into and out of the central city. The effect would be the same for Watts in either case.

Mr. Harrington mentions the recommendation of the conference of mayors that the Federal government withhold funds for community facilities and education unless the recipient community (especially the suburban community) agrees to take a reasonable share of low-cost housing and low-income pupils. One could wish that the mayors were as public-minded as their statement suggests. It seems to me, rather, that they were doing what big-city mayors have done for some time, and not unreasonably—namely, attempting to foist a share of the social problems of the urban poor (especially Negroes) on the suburban communities that evade them. But they were not acting primarily out of concern for social justice; their chief concern was for city revenues, city services, and the preservation of peace and placidity in the ghettos. In short, I question the assertion that social accounting will restrain the middle classes from "imposing their private tastes upon the common good." For it is the private tastes of the middle classes that form the substance of what America sees as the common good—including the automobile, the suburban home, and the abandonment of the city.

The use of political subdivisions to maintain social and economic inequalities is a fundamental problem, as Mr. Harrington observes, and he looks hopefully to area-wide (or regional) planning as offering a way out. However, I think a good case can be made that the city and its poor will be victimized by new regional configurations, and I am currently at work preparing that case in collaboration with my colleague, Professor Frances Piven.

Suburban communities have long resisted regionalism because they fear both the domination by the central city and the invasion by its poor, especially its black poor; furthermore, great resistance comes from their wish to avoid having to share the cost of rehabilitating the city. It is reasonable to expect that all this resistance will wane as suburban areas come to perceive that they, not the cities, will have the upper hand in regional relations. The continuing rapid population growth of the suburbs, coupled with the Supreme Court's reapportionment decision, will soon make such dominance possible. Thus, regionalism shortly may not only be embraced by suburban leaders, but also may become the *technical* vehicle by which suburban whites can reassert political control over the city and its swelling black population. This represents the contemporary re-enactment of an earlier political strategem when successive waves of municipal reform represented efforts by the Protestant corporate establishment to recapture the city from the political machines of the Catholic immigrant masses. If the suburbs win, we will then get programs to revitalize and rehabilitate the cities. And it is not difficult to imagine the values that will be reflected in programs promulgated by suburban interests. They will be good programs—for the white middle classes (as urban renewal has been); but they will not meet the needs of the poor and the dispossessed.

The question, then, is not how accounting and planning will benefit the poor, but how the poor can protect themselves from this new technology—a technology which threatens to victimize them all the more. How can they see to it that their interests are also plugged into the computerized processing of facts and figures? This question is especially important at a time when the possibilities for influence by the poor are being affected by substantial changes in American life:

1. The poor have become a numerical minority; thus, their capability for exerting electoral influence has diminished.

2. Vast corporate power has become a new and decisive influence on electoral processes and on government; but the poor possess no corporate resources.

3. The small, remaining economic leverage of the poor—that almost indispensable source of political influence—is now decreasing; so many are in dispersed and marginal occupations that they are increasingly vulnerable to replacement by the machine.

How, then, are the poor to be organized? How is the political vitality for a new thrust against social and economic inequality to be generated? How can the poor exercise some influence over the professional bureaucracies where social accounting will be done? These are the real questions before us. To ignore these questions— while advocating an expansion of technical and professional planning devices—is hardly to advance the cause of social injustice. It is merely to turn away once again from the grim necessity of finding political solutions to political problems.

COMMENTARY

JOHN B. TURNER

I.

Michael Harrington's assertion that the leadership of this country proposes making a social revolution but without the inconvenience of changing any basic institutions, constitutes perhaps the sharpest criticism that can be made about the wars on poverty and racial injustice. The central assumption in this assertion is that colored and poor minorities cannot lose the handicaps imposed on them by their status without the help of social institutions. Furthermore, these institutions cannot provide the help that is required to fit the reality of the American way of life to the promise of the American dream, without undergoing some major changes themselves.

Revolutions can be classified according to their purpose into two types: first, those that seek to deal with a malignant social situation. Such revolutions seek to do away with the existing social order, its institutions, its centers of power, and the class of people who symbolize the status quo. The assumption is that the status quo is malignant and the only answer is to cut out the old social growth and to let a new, vigorous, and healthy social order take over. This is perhaps the common concept of a revolution, and yet it is repulsive to many Americans who, though critical of some aspect of American life, nevertheless hold tremendous confidence in its past accomplishments and its future promise.

But Mr. Harrington has reference to a second type of revolution, which seeks to change a social order conceded to be basically healthy yet in need of rejuvenation, and the existing social order itself is capable of generating the necessary changes. In such revolutions, it is assumed that there will be conflict. It is further assumed that the harmful elements of conflict can be constrained within a super bond of unity and purpose. This position views the defenders of the status quo and the advocates of change as constantly changing groups—depending upon the issues and the knowledge of the consequences of policy. Likewise, it assumes that the same people who are opposed on some issues will be allies on others. In this type of revolution, which I shall call *the benign revolution*, the in-group and the out-group are co-managers of change.

It is important to distinguish the benign revolution from an evolutionary process. Among other things, revolution rejects gradualism. It seeks major change, even reversal of direction of policy and behavior. The benign revolution effects these changes, perhaps not instantly, but at least within the enjoyable lifetime of the present population.

President Johnson's statement about the objective of the Great Society, to make "a place where men are more concerned with the quality of their goals than with the quantity of their goods," is often quoted by Mr. Harrington as one definition of the goals of the current social revolution which must be taken seriously. The struggle for quality of life versus its quantifiable aspects is indeed very old. But, as Mr. Harrington points out, for the first time in history perhaps, the level of wealth in this country is such that we can afford to seek quality not just for the poor and for the racial and ethnic minorities, but, indeed, for all Americans. Thus the responsibility to pursue social policy toward enhancing the quality of life for all citizens is more incumbent upon our leaders than ever before.

What are the requirements for conducting this benign revolution successfully? Mr. Harrington makes a case for establishing first a system of social accounting as an integral part of the making of social policy. He means by this, a deliberate, scientifically oriented public investigation of the social consequences of present and projected public policy. He has argued superbly the need of reversing the eroding public expression of the concept of Equality—which he views as a fundamental cornerstone of public policy. In an era of affluence, we are challenged to discard outmoded measures of justice and to find a more just system of distributing our wealth. Of special note is his point that achievement of Equality will require a partial or compensatory re-allocation of resources to help those who are disadvantaged by past inequities in the social system.

It is difficult to disagree with the importance and salience of these two conditions—social accounts and a rediscovered sense of egalitarianism. But how are they to be brought about? In my opinion, Mr. Harrington provides us with cogent insight. He states that "the quality of life has become a political question." At first, this statement sounds like an old axiom repeated in every era of our history. But I believe he meant much more; for not only do some citizens have substantially less quality in their lives than others, but there is the growing possibility that the quality of life for all citizens is increasingly threatened. Today, the scope of a citizen's dependency upon others for the satisfaction of basic needs and wants is more pervasive than ever before, thus making him increasingly vulnerable to the decisions and actions of others; not just others whom he knows and with whom he interacts personally, but the *impersonal others* to whom he may very well remain invisible, nameless, numberless, locationless—an abstract part of a mass society.

Therefore, we may conclude that at the very heart of what Mr. Harrington has to say is his belief that the primary arena for action to improve the quality of life is the political arena. This means that many issues once considered a matter of private interest are now a matter of public interest; issues once considered of local interest are now also matters of regional and national interest and therefore subject to public policy at local, regional, and national levels. It implies that the once divergent goals and means of individuals and vested-interest groups will require deliberate transformation to accurately reflect the interests of the commonweal.

II.

Mr. Harrington advocates the use of knowledge of the consequences of public decisions and the use of values as tools in shaping public policy. He expresses enormous confidence in the rationality of the public. But the dictates of knowledge frequently are not followed in matters of private (or public) interest. Therefore, have we reason to believe that knowledge alone of the consequences of a particular policy dealing with mass transit, for example, will cause the voters to behave any differently than they might without that knowledge? Or, have we reason to believe that knowledge of the consequences of alternative levels of support for public education will cause the voters to select a level of support on a rational basis? The questions to which the makers of social change must find answers are—under what conditions will a system of social accounts be effective as a tool toward rational social policy? Under what conditions will values lead to public decisions which contribute to the quality of life improvement?

Political analysts observe that "in ordinary circumstances voters cannot be expected to transcend their particular localized and self-regarding opinions." They suggest that the sum of the opinions or lack of opinions of a plurality of voters does not automatically produce sound public policy. It would seem that it is not that men have different public interests, living as interdependently as we do, but rather that each person lives with a plurality of competing private and special interests often at odds with the public interest.

Public interest may be defined as "what men would choose if they saw clearly, thought rationally, acted disinterestedly and benevolently." But some political analysts do not agree that the public interest can be determined *a priori*; they hold that the public interest is what emerges from the struggle of political decision of competing groups and that only in this way can the factors which determine rationality be properly weighed and taken into account.

The *a priori* determination of public interest emphasizes the importance of knowledge and values. The second point of view emphasizes the utility of power and influence. Actually these two approaches to deciding the public interest, while representing divergent ideas, do not clash head-on, but together they present a clearer picture of the factors which go into the formulation of public policy.

Although the methodology and perhaps even the ideology of the benign revolution are not entirely clear and precise, Mr. Harrington's paper has suggested the general course that action must take. It is clear that any successful effort toward a benign social revolution must encompass multiple strategies and resources. But perhaps some strategies are more important than others in that they are a prerequisite for others. For example, his insistence on egalitarianism regained might constitute one of the conditions for successfully using a system of social accounts. The strategy suggested here is one of concerting those groups with political influence who are ready to practice egalitarianism on a particular issue. But if the practice of egalitarianism is as fragile as Mr. Harrington thinks it to be, a prior condition must be the strengthening of the practice of social justice.

Significant gains in this area will surely require an initial success in overcoming the gross inequities in legitimate forms of social power of disadvantaged groups, thus enabling the imbalance in political, economic, and social bargaining to be corrected or, at least, to be significantly offset. To accomplish this would achieve a more equal distribution of the profit of some present public policies and increase the receptivity of some groups in our society to the concept of egalitarianism.

I do not consider the development of functional power by the poor and other disadvantaged minorities a sufficient condition to release them from their second class status, but it is clearly a necessary condition. It is somewhat paradoxical that these citizens must acquire their relative independence at a time in history when, although the country's resources and productivity are greater than ever before, there is a realistic shrinking of access to opportunity for them. Under such conditions the earning of functional power is made much more difficult, and while it is true that power is seldom transferred as an altruistic gift, it is precisely around this issue that the in-group can act to make it possible for the acquisition of functional power to take place. It is precisely at this point that we make the benign revolution a reality or a myth.

But who, among the in-group, is to take the initiative? What is the division of labor to be? Who is going to direct the benign revolution? Who is prepared to enter the political arena and aggressively re-define and seek the public interest? Who is prepared to work for the conditions which will lead to a correction of the imbalance of functional power? Mr. Harrington's paper was not addressed to these questions. Indeed, in all probability there are no ready made answers in any meaningful sense. The answers are the cutting edge of the future.

In conclusion, I would like to make two brief observations which have some bearing on these questions.

First, if social work as a profession—as a field of service to people, as an important area of volunteer work, as a sector of the educational enterprise—is to play an important part in the conduct of the benign revolution, social work itself must undergo change and inconvenience. Some critics of social work say that this change is not possible. Time does not permit here a discussion of the nature of this change. But whether public or voluntary, lay or staff, the welfare establishment needs to do combat with the notions that it cannot bring about major changes internal to itself. Failure to do so is to admit inability to carry out in microcosm what is needed to carry out the larger benign social revolution. It seems to me that Mr. Harrington's thesis, in particular, offers a challenge to the layman. At this moment, voluntaryism is in trouble as a result of its incapacity to deal with conflict between private interests and public interest, between sectarian interests and non-sectarian interests. The layman and voluntaryism must join hands to help create incentives to work for public interest while helping to maintain those areas of thought and action which can legitimately remain within the domain of private interests.

Second and finally, if a system of social accounting is to be established, the role of the technician is going to expand and will become more crucial in public decision-making matters. For example, mayors and city and county managers will increasingly need staffs of able assistants skilled in laying out alternative ways of doing things and skilled in specifying the social consequences of a particular course of action, not in the narrow traditional terms of professional references but in terms of the social costs and gains in all areas of human life. This means that the training of engineers, economists, doctors, social workers, school administrators, and many other professionals must undergo changes to accommodate these new demands. For certainly Mr. Harrington's paper has made clear the need for a new force in contemporary American democracy, namely, a class of professionals who are rational thinkers, capable of and biased towards disinterested action and committed to a public philosophy of freedom, brotherhood, and egalitarianism.

COMMENTARY

ALTON A. LINFORD

I am honored to have been invited to be a discussant of Mr. Harrington's paper. We honor him as the man who precipitated the current national sympathetic interest in the poor which has stimulated so much recent social legislation related to the Great Society.

While one has to agree with Mr. Harrington that the gap is wide between President Johnson's proposals and his eloquent expression of the goals of the Great Society, in fairness one must acknowledge that the accomplishment is also considerable. One might say that the achievement suffers only by comparison with the eloquence. Even a listing of the major legislation related to the Great Society concept indicates a solid accomplishment in social programming. It has been rivaled, if at all, only by the New Deal record in the years 1933 to 1937. One need only mention such major programs as the Economic Opportunity Act, the Area Redevelopment programs, Medicare, Federal aid to education (both to elementary and secondary, and to higher education), the Civil Rights Act of 1965, the Mental Retardation Facilities and Community Mental Health Centers Construction Act, the heart, cancer, and stroke programs, the Manpower Development and Training Act, not to speak of the numerous amendments of continuing social welfare programs, to realize that the accomplishment has been truly phenomenal. If the pace of the past four years can be maintained, even the most avid actionist will have no cause for complaint.

I am pleased that Mr. Harrington takes an optimistic view of the "Great Society" as something that is attainable, not just "pie in the sky." This attitude—that society is perfectible—has permitted philosophers, dreamers, planners, social workers to continue to produce plans and prescriptions for achieving utopia.

Mr. Harrington's prescription for achieving the Great Society contains three elements: (1) adopting equality rather than minimum standards as our goal, (2) abandoning the profit motive, and finally (3) developing and utilizing a system of social accounting.

Time does not permit comment on all three points, so I will address my remarks to the concept of social accounting. Mr. Harrington's proposals concerning equality and the profit motive are matters on which reasonable people can and have differed. In my view they both involve more a question of faith and morals than of measurable or demonstrable fact.

That we might devise a system of accounts, a series of measurements, a collection of tools that would provide us with adequate and reliable data for social planning and for social assessment is a dream that we have had for a very long time. The thought that it might be possible to develop a measurement, a kind of national fever chart that would record the national social well-being, a device that would reveal with unfailing accuracy the social pathologies and the socially healthy areas of society, is heady stuff indeed. Another fascinating potential of social accounting is that one might measure or predict the social consequences of the adoption of a given public policy or the initiation of a given industrial or business enterprise.

Whether such dramatic results are possible or not, it is certain that much could be accomplished if we were to direct enough of our resources—brains and money—toward this end. Indeed, it is my contention that we have made beginnings in the development of some of the essential ingredients of social accounting in the last three and a half decades. I refer to the progress made in measuring and reporting such things as family income, population estimates and projections, welfare expenditures, unemployment and labor force data, health and disablement data, and housing.

Despite such advancement, however, this country is still forced to make most important social policy decisions on the basis of grossly inadequate data. For this and other reasons, policy and program "decisions are made piecemeal, often without regard to context or to the effect on other decisions." It is no wonder, then, that our social policies and programs often produce unintended and unforeseen consequences.

Numerous examples come to mind. By focusing too narrowly on

public low-cost housing without regard to side effects, we have created monstrous collections of problem families in segregated neighborhoods. Having assembled multiple problem families in these areas, we then supply them with schools, churches, neighborhood houses, and commercial shops, so that residents of these places experience a kind of institutional life, rarely venturing outside this closed community of problem families. The social costs of this development must be great, but they have never been measured.

We create a system of public assistance designed to provide income to a residual group of needy families until other measures such as social insurance and public work can absorb them and do the whole job. Having concerned ourselves too exclusively with the problem of providing income to needy people, we have overlooked the social consequences of programs which merely maintain millions of people in poverty with little concern for those elements which spell opportunity and upward movement—programs which because of their "means test" base, rob recipients of incentive, of hope, often of self-respect. What are the social consequences or costs of forcing eight million people to prove their inadequacy over and over again: their inability to find or hold a job or otherwise support themselves, their lack of husbands or fathers to support them, or the fact that they are too ill or too disabled to work? If by chance an assistance recipient earns some money, we insist on deducting it from the budget, and so we leave him no better off for having bothered to get a job. Even when we exempt a portion of the public-assistance recipient's earnings, we diminish the incentive to self-support.

Clearly we need a system of social accounting which will permit an overview of the whole range of social well-being and/or social pathology, and a way of assessing the total social effect of a proposed program or policy change. It might be argued that we should not require a full and accurate social accounting in order to persuade us to abandon such obviously costly and fallacious programs. However, there are no signs that we intend to abandon these policies and practices.

Compared with progress in other areas of society—industrial technology and economic analysis, for example—we are indeed laggard in social analysis and social accounting. However, despite limited investment in this area, dramatic progress has been made in the last thirty years.

In 1931, when some courageous souls were advocating Federal aid for the needy unemployed, and President Hoover was assuring the country that the American way (voluntarism) was equal to the task, we lacked any nationwide data on the number of unemployed, the number of persons on public and private relief, and the amounts of money spent. The only country-wide data were those gathered by the Children's Bureau from a few major cities. When Grace Abbott, Chief of the Children's Bureau, reported that 66 per cent of relief funds in 1931 came from tax sources, Mr. Hoover, expressing great skepticism, asked the Bureau of the Census to get the facts. It was found that the Children's Bureau meager facts were the only ones available. Since then, of course, we've developed an effective system of fact-gathering and analysis of both the recipients of public aid and the dollars spent—first by the Federal Emergency Relief Administration and later by the Social Security Board and its successors in the Department of Health, Education and Welfare. It should be noted, however, that when the Social Security Act was passed in 1935, it was based on very meager social data.

Throughout the depression years of the 1930's, when unemployment was widespread, the country lacked even reasonably accurate measures of the extent and nature of unemployment. The beginnings of such measurements had to await the 1940's when a system of reporting and analysis was devised in connection with the employment service and unemployment compensation.

It will be recalled that with the creation of the Children's Bureau in 1912, the country was provided with one of the first governmental-research agencies for the study of social problems. Its early studies related to infant mortality, child labor, juvenile delinquency, and child dependency—each of which stimulated important national and state legislation designed to correct the ills revealed. But again, both the research and the corrective measures were piecemeal and too often unrelated to the whole social fabric.

Meanwhile, however, the systems of fact-gathering and social measurement have been pushed ahead by various units in the Department of Health, Education and Welfare, the Labor Department, the Census Bureau, and the Department of Housing and Urban Development.

The facts are, however, that almost all our current governmental fact-finding and social research continue to be related to single and specific problems and programs, with few, if any, attempts to achieve an overview of the country's well-being and of the total effect of a program innovation. Child welfare is a case in point. As pointed out by Professor Alfred J. Kahn, instead of approaching the welfare of children from the overall viewpoint of their needs as members of families, we have approached it in terms of *child* welfare, which implies such fragmented services as foster care, adoptions, and protective services. In the words of the National Commission on Technology, Automation, and Economic Progress, "We do not have, as yet, a continuous charting of social changes, and we have been ill-prepared (in such matters as housing, education, or the status of the Negro) to determine our needs, establish goals and measure our performance. Lacking any systematic assessment, we have few criteria which allow us to test the effectiveness of present policies or weigh alternatives regarding future programs."

The National Commission's proposal is that a governmental agency, perhaps the Council of Economic Advisers, be asked to develop a system of social accounting, similar to one already developed in the national economic accounting, to "give us a broader and more balanced reckoning of the meaning of social and economic progress" and to "move us toward measurement of the utilization of human resources in our society."

I do not believe that anyone fully grasps the reach and significance of the concept of social accounting. Its effectiveness and practical use must await more study. The National Commission, however, has asserted its usefulness in the following four areas:

(1) The measurement of social costs and net returns of economic innovation, such as: the benefits and costs of a new industry, or a new product, or perhaps a new plant located in a given community; the social cost of air or water pollution, or the requirement that labor be imported, or that public roads or other facilities be built.

(2) The measurement of social ills: such things as the social and economic cost of crime, mental illness, desertion, unemployment, illness, illiteracy, or segregated education.

(3) The creation of performance budgets or measurements that

would reliably tell us how well our society is performing in such matters as providing needed medical and health service to everyone, or adequate housing, or education, or mental health.

(4) Indicators of economic opportunity and social mobility, for example: an index indicating the status and well-being of the Negro in United States society. Just what is his status? How is it improving in relation to his educational level, lifetime earnings, employment opportunities, freedom to work and live where he chooses?

Other areas in which the social-accounting tool might be useful include: evolution of current social-welfare programs, assessment of social-welfare manpower needs, and the projection of results of consequences of adoption of a proposed social policy or program innovation.

I believe this country should proceed to develop and utilize a system of social accounting with all possible dispatch. In doing so we should make maximum use of all academic disciplines and professions and all the technology and methods of study available to us—including computers, systems analysis, and operations research. We cannot afford to make less than maximum use of these devices to develop effective tools for social planning and social policy and program assessment.

In urging this course of action, however, I want to note some cautions. Great as are the potential results of social accounting, there are also potential hazards and social losses. I will note three such:

(1) There is a large subjective value component to all social programs and policies. Assessment of programs and identification of so-called pathological conditions require assumptions about objectives and purposes of programs and policies and about what constitutes a state of well-being. (For example, one might infer from Mr. Harrington's paper that possession of wealth is as pathologic as poverty.) Creation of any system of social assessment must scrupulously avoid imposing a system of values that runs counter to our democratic ethic and the rights of individuals. It might prove to be impossible to develop a full-blown system of social accounting without invading the thicket of individual values and ethics.

(2) In creating this system of social accounting, we must endeavor to build into it safeguards that will prevent the misuse of information and data about individual people that will be assembled.

(For example, in order to accomplish the potential of this system it may be necessary to assemble extensive factual data about every person in our society, including his behavior, preferences, attitudes, and associates. One's imagination does not have to range far to conceive ways in which political organizations, legislative investigating committees, and demagogues might exploit such information, if they were permitted access to it.) It will be imperative to build into the system foolproof safeguards against the use of such information to embarrass or harass a person.

(3) It should be observed that many of the measurements contemplated in this system of social accounting will be no sounder than the adequacy and accuracy of the data on which they are based. Inaccurate data fed into a computer will not produce correct answers, no matter how suitable the questions. Perhaps the problem may be sharpened by an example: measuring the social cost of unemployment. Accurate data perhaps could be obtained on wage loss, on benefit payments under unemployment compensation and public assistance, and on loss of gross national product. But how can one hope to obtain accurate data on the costs of family tension, school drop-out, ill health, and crime resulting from unemployment? It can be argued validly, of course, that we do not need to measure such costs with precision in order to make a decision to eliminate unemployment. My caution remains, however: social measurement and prediction should be used with caution unless and until necessary data can be obtained on an accurate basis.

Let us get on with the development of a system of social accounting, but let us use it with discretion until it is tested and proven.

THE RESPONSE

MICHAEL HARRINGTON

Now let me begin this quite brief response with a couple of general comments which relate to some statements by Dean Linford. First of all, this is not really a complete description of my utopia that I presented today but only a small part of it. I hope that nobody thinks this is all I want to do. Many of the criticisms made by all of the discussants, I think, relate to this limitation. I've got all kinds of blueprints in my pockets and social accounting and my other proposals are only openers.

Second, I do think it is important to recognize achievement. As a matter of fact, in every speech that I've given since the President declared the "war on poverty," despite all of my criticisms, I've always said and still say that there has been an enormous gain, that John Kennedy and Lyndon Johnson put the topics of poverty and social change on the table. So I am aware of the achievements. The one thing I would stress, though, is that the achievements also have to be measured in terms of the profundity of the crisis. It seems to me that the alternatives are not a Great Society on the one hand or a semi–Great Society on the other. The alternatives are, as I said before, either a Great Society or 1984 and the Brave New World.

Specifically, I absolutely agree with Dr. Cloward that, in the wrong hands, all the techniques which I advocate can be used against the very people with whom I'm concerned. Galbraith has coined the phrase "reactionary Keynesianism" to describe "Keynesianism" used precisely to promote inequality in profit. I think there is such a thing. I think social accounts could be used by shrewd, manipulative bureaucrats, corporation-type rationalizers, or social engineers to make an absolutely miserable society. Perhaps I didn't stress enough the decisive thing that I have to add, and Dr. Cloward is right to tax me on this point. I want to stress now that my ideas will work only if there's a democratic, political movement—a political movement, imposing, out of people's actions and choices and participations, values upon these systems of social accounting.

As a matter of fact, I would say that the American problem today politically, is the lack of a democratic left. We are, so to speak, a country which has a right wing and a center, but not a democratic left. In rational terms, President Johnson and his consensus politics really should be in the center. There should be a mass movement to the left of that—a democratic, small "d" movement. I'm not putting down the Democratic Party, which I generally tend to support, but I just want to emphasize that I'm talking about the emergence in the society of a democratic, political movement, of a democratic left, as a pre-condition for the validity of any of my ideas. I completely agree with Dr. Cloward, therefore, that the social organization of the poor, their self-organization, and their making alliances with other forces of society is an absolute prerequisite.

Therefore, I accept Dr. Turner's analysis of the "benign revolution," as long as I can make the benignity a little bit more nasty than Dr. Turner's designation. That is to say, I agree that there must be shifting alliances in any political movement that's going to do the things I advocate. I agree that the old Marxist idea of the proletariat—as an overwhelming, monolithic, major democratic force—is now irrelevant. It would be much simpler in a sense if it existed, but it doesn't. Now social change is a question of coalitions and alliances among disparate forces. The religious movement, the trade unions, the Negroes, the liberals, the educated, all these people who have conflicts as well as unity, must form a coalition. I would agree with Dr. Turner on this point, but I would emphasize—here's where I want to be even a little nastier—that all of these alliances have to come to a new movement, something so new that it will challenge basic institutions in the society.

Some people are going to lose, like automobile corporations, I hope. And I'm sure they're going to be unhappy, but I want to beat them with this movement within a democratic framework and I think only a democratic movement challenging that corporate institution can get us to a sane transportation policy. Also I strongly support Dr. Turner's important point that the problems we are talking about do not affect simply the poor, or the workers, or the central city dweller—these things corrupt the entire society. In New York, for example, the middle class and the rich in Manhattan are absolutely outraged that they can't walk in Central Park. Their park has been taken away from them. This change has been a social cost to the middle class and the wealthy for the injustices we perpetrate on people. But, in any case, I agree completely with Dr. Turner, that this is something that involves more than the middle class. And yet I want to stress to the middle class specifically that they're involved in these problems too—the entire society is involved.

Now, finally, a few more points on Dean Linford's reply. In terms of equality, I was really thinking more of ethos rather than the practice of income distribution. Let me put it very simply—

I've spent fair amounts of time in Europe and there is a profound difference between an American waiter and a British waiter. Part of that difference is the egalitarian ethos of the society. The American waiter has a sense of his own dignity, a very profound and good thing, which he draws from our civilization. So strong is our egalitarian ethos at times that we kid ourselves into denying the class stratifaction that actually exists, and this is a problem in itself. Unfortunately there are some workers and poor people who say, "I'm just as good as Henry Ford," which is true in one sense, but not in another.

What I'm talking about then, really, is this *feel* of egalitarianism in America. I don't want to go extensively into what I am for, but I'm certainly not for simply distributing the wealth in America to everybody share by share. I'm for creating a new kind of society in the long run; but in the short run, all I'm saying is that at a bare minimum Federal government policies should not promote inequality with tax funds. I don't think this idea is very utopian or radical. The government at least should not be pushing inequality; the government should fight it.

Two final points on Dean Linford's comments. First, on the revision of the welfare means test, I think the present information is absolutely sufficient. I don't think we need a bit more data. We should revise right now, and there are serious proposals being made to do so. I have personally long been in favor of the idea of guaranteeing, as a fundamental right in this society, a living income to every American. An income, let me hasten to add, which gives the individual the right to go out and spend it on drink and gambling and women if that's his choice. A minimum income is not going to solve all problems, but I think we're rich enough and creative enough now to put a floor over abject misery.

Second, I think there are more hopeful avenues for developing data on relations between unemployment and various intangibles. For example, we now have the whole dispute over the Moynihan Report which, God knows, I don't want to raise here at this hour, but simply to point out that here serious study has been given to the relationship between, let us say, divorce and the break-up of the home and the unemployment rate. This year's Manpower Report gives some rather flat statements that in certain slum areas, as unemployment decreases by a given percentage, there is an almost predictable correlation of the decrease of divorce and the break-up of homes. I agree that information has to be used with caution, but I think there's great hope here.

Let me try to conclude with the main point that I would like to emphasize. There will be no fulfillment of these values and proposals unless there is a dynamic, mass, democratic movement; unless the kind of spirit and *élan* and participation that has characterized the Negro non-violent movement because a general characteristic of a broad, majority social movement. That's the pre-condition. Because it seems to me, and Dr. Cloward has a very important point, we are going to get some kind of planning in the future. We are going to get some kind of social accounting in the future, because this interdependent society requires both the good guys and the bad guys to plan and account. The issue is not whether or not we're going to have this planning—the really fundamental issue is what *kind* of planning, with what *values* as a base. Will it be the bureaucratic mode that Dr. Cloward speaks about, in which middle-class people and administrators impose their values on people, or will it be something else? The crucial dimension to me is the political dimension and the emergence of a democratic left in the United States. In conclusion, then, those concerned with social theory and invention, those concerned with social work and social action, must also in the most profound and active sense be concerned with politics and the emergence of a new political, social movement in the United States.

III

THE ESSAY

Captives, Consensus and Conflict: Implications for New Roles in Social Change

MELVIN TUMIN

Professor of Sociology and Anthropology, Princeton University

COMMENTARY

EUGEN PUSIĆ

Professor of Public Administration, Zagreb University (Yugoslavia); President, International Conference of Social Work

LUCIEN MEHL

President of the Technical School for Factory and Social Service Superintendents (Viroflay, France)

IRVING ROSOW

Professor of Social Work, School of Applied Social Sciences, Case Western Reserve University

THE RESPONSE

MELVIN TUMIN

Captives, Consensus and Conflict:
Implications for New Roles in Social Change

MELVIN TUMIN

If there should be any who doubt that customs change with time, or who insist that in any event the more things change, the more they remain the same, consider this particular bit of law governing relations in the family during the colonial period in American history: "If a man have a stubborn and rebellious son of sufficient years and understanding, viz: sixteen years of age, which will not obey the voice of his father or the voice of his mother, and that when they have chastised him will not hearken unto them, then may his father and mother, being his natural parents, lay hold on him and bring him to the magistrates assembled in court, and testify unto them that their son is stubborn and rebellious ... such a son shall be put to death." [1]

It does not matter that there are no reported instances of this law having been applied literally. What is important is that since those days, and with every turn of the generations, significant shifts in power relations within basic institutions have been characteristic of American society. Roles have been redefined, including whole new sets of rights and responsibilities, which, had they been promulgated or even suggested at an earlier time, would have been considered utterly outlandish and totally unworkable. Even the law, being chronically slow to change, especially when basic social relationships such as those between parent and child or between spouses were at stake, has been recodified in every generation. The seventeenth-century rule that no single person, male or female, could live alone in the State of Connecticut shortly thereafter came to be considered

---

[1] Cited by W. Goodsell, A *History of Marriage and the Family* (New York: The Macmillan Co., 1934), p. 367.

foolish and meaningless; and, of course, today's children would taunt without respite such a norm of conduct as prescribed in an eighteenth-century New England book of etiquette, which admonished children "Never sit down at the table till asked, and after the blessing. Ask for nothing; tarry till it be offered thee. Speak not. Sing not, hum not, wriggle not. . . . When any speak to thee, stand up. . . ." [2]

Some such historical perspective is needed by every adult generation to prepare it for drastic changes during its own lifetime. Our generation, of course, is no exception. Yet we seem as unprepared to accept the insurgencies characteristic of our times as any previous generation. Whatever else may be said of us in times to come, let no one doubt that we are as persistently parochial as any who have come before us.

This parochialism will do us no good, of course. For there is an ineluctability and relentlessness about the pressures toward new role definitions that can hardly be denied. Perhaps it might be the better part of sociological wisdom to play out our traditional roles of resisters and square old hats, so that the new modes and styles of relationships will be somewhat less radically different than they would be had we not mustered countervailing power. But this is to be decided only from the perspective of different sets of values, held by the contestants, in this very large and endless social game.

In any event, it is undeniable that basic changes are in process: changes in role relationships between parents and children, spouses, teachers and students, doctors and patients, Negroes and Whites, poor nations and rich nations, here in this country and everywhere.

What is perhap unique to our time and place is the extent to which the balance of *power* in these relationships has been made an explicit issue. This is surprising, for it can hardly be doubted any longer that a crucial and defining feature of the style and content of any relationship is the way in which power—the capacity to realize one's own ends, even against opposition—is distributed among the actors involved.

That power is central to human relationships, is given first, in a formal way, by the very definition of a relationship, i.e., a purposeful

[2] From A. W. Calhoun, *Social History of the American Family*, I (New York: Barnes and Noble, 1960), pp. 112–13.

interaction between people. For where there are actors with purposes that each intends to realize in the relationship, then the differential capacity to achieve one's intentions, even against opposition, clearly becomes a crucial facet of the relationship.

Whether the relationship is transacted within the network of kinship, economic, educational or religious rules and roles; whether love, socialization, child rearing, profit or eternal salvation are at stake; whether the players are many or few; whether electronic mass media or crude sign language are the principle means of communication—in any and all of these situations and structures, what will be accomplished and how it will come to pass depends critically on who has the capacity to enforce his will.

The emergence of power considerations into open focus has generated two very significant negative reactions. The first is a frequent and intense moral outrage which censures those relationships that are nakedly and almost solely political. (We in the Western world have clearly developed a central common theme of regret and disdain for the use of power in an undisguised fashion —however much in fact we may secretly adore it and its possessors and turn ourselves over to them on demand.) The second reaction, corollary of the first, is our insistence that even when the situation calls for matching brute power against brute power in a struggle that means defeat and death for one of the parties (as in a war for example), there shall be rules that serve to some degree to mitigate or restrict the full utilization of relevant power. Rules of warfare constitute as anomalous and ambivalent a moral posture as we have ever invented; rules governing prize fights are only somewhat less so. Yet we insist on these ritualistic sugar-coatings in a vain effort to deceive ourselves into believing that we are thereby civilized. Perhaps in fact we are really showing how much we fear unlimited power, not so much because it corrupts, which it does, but because it destroys, which it does even more. In general, almost any modality other than power is considered superior to power—at least morally; and therefore, where power has to be asserted, the relationship is viewed as having deteriorated.

Such dim views of power and the consequent efforts to hedge its use, testify, we argue, to our perception of its ubiquity and its ability to drive out all other modes of relationship unless otherwise restrained. In these regards, power and sex are very much alike in our consciousness.

Some argue against the notion that power is central in human relationships by pointing to the occasions when there are stalemates in power. But such stalemates testify only that there is ignorance regarding the actual unequal distribution of power, or that only a momentary equilibrium has been reached. And if the capacity to decide moves from party to party in such transactions, this is evidence not of the irrelevance of power but rather of its shifting balance from phase to phase in the relationship.

Others who are inclined to give power a secondary role sometimes defend this position by arguing that the way power is distributed "all depends"—sometimes on money, other times on love, or law, or even skill in deception. But to assert power's dependence is to identify the variety of possible sources of power and not the subordinacy of the term in some conceptual or explanatory scheme. If I refrain from exercising the fullness of my legal powers to get my son to do as I wish because I desire that he shall also love me or respect me, I am in fact deliberately reducing the gross power available for the one end of filial obedience to achieve competing ends of filial love and respect.

Having now argued on behalf of the scope and significance of power in human relationships, some caveats must immediately be entered. First, to say that power is crucial and defining in social relationships is not to say that those relationships are nothing but exchanges of power. If power shapes the style and content of a relationship that is not the same as saying that power is all there is to that style and content. Second, if love, money, or prestige can and do serve as variable sources of power, so, in turn, does power serve as a source of love, money, and prestige. Indeed, the interplay of so-called dependent and independent variables may be such that one would do better to think in terms of continuous reciprocal interaction among such variables rather than in terms of straight line causal sequences marked by time units. At one and the same moment we can and do use power, money, love and fame to help accumulate each other. In short, no naïve reductionism or simple-minded model of cause and effect is being suggested or implied here.

It is also relevant to issue the caution that certain quotients of ignorance, error and deception are often indispensable to the maintenance and health of social relationships such as between parent and child, husband and wife, neighbor and neighbor. One must always be reflective, therefore, about how explicit the power ingredient should be and how aware and conscious of this dimension the participants ought to become. For certain purposes, it may be much wiser to withhold power, minimize its relevance, and suppress consciousness of its significance. If, therefore, we now press hard to make very explicit just how power does function and how significant it can be, this is not to be taken as advocating that social relationships should always be altered to give power more conscious prominence.

If power is ubiquitous, variable, consequential and unequally distributed in most social relationships, it also tends as such to be deeply institutionalized and self-perpetuating. Those who control relationships are not notorious for the ease with which they share or surrender that control. Moreover, they are usually in a position to manufacture appropriate ideologies to rationalize the status quo of power distribution and to repress contrary ideologies. If they have enough power, they can even repress knowledge of the possibility of alternatives, without which discontent may be ancient and endemic, but inconsequential.

There is an interesting flexibility and adaptability of the styles of rationales and ideologies that justify unequal power. Within the last three hundred years we have lived through the notions of the divine right of kings, the natural inferiority of certain races and peoples, and of the corollary idea of the white man's burden in the many forms in which it has been expressed. While all of these are still with us in one form or another, however attenuated or *sotto voce* they may be in their mode of expression, we have acquired still others, more appropriate to modern industrial society. These include the theory of bureaucracy, which emphasizes the supreme value of efficiency and the requirement of unequal power for efficient management. Most egregious here is the example of the almost unquestioned acceptance of the necessity for total inequality in the military bureaucracy and in certain orthodox institutionalized religions. In these cases, the basic appeal is to the welfare of the institution as a whole, a vaguely defined and nebulous non-organism, whose existence and magically endowed living properties are invoked by the gate-keepers at the appropriate moments, to defend the unequally distributed rights to decide how that institution shall function. Like all appeals to the needs and wishes of non-empirically verifiable entities, questions regarding the decisions of those in control are feckless since there is no one to whom to appeal.

Perhaps most widespread of all today is that rationale which rests the claim of entitlement to superior power upon the supposedly greater wisdom, experience, skill, or knowledge of the powerful. This is a beguiling rationale, for the powerful almost always insist that they use their power in the best interests of the powerless. Under this rubric we find such relationships as that between doctor and patient, parent and child, teacher and pupil, social worker and client, majority group and immigrant group, and rich nation and poor nation. Paternalism in these relationships is usually explicitly acknowledged and, if a "liberal conscience" happens to plague the powerful, the paternalism is sometimes explicitly regretted, but, nevertheless, asserted as unavoidable and required for the best interests of all concerned.

In the face of these claims, one cannot help but reflect that if we were to believe all the people, groups and nations who assert that they are doing things only out of the best of motives and almost solely on behalf of the interests of others, we should find ourselves in a world dominated by fanatically altruistic and selfless people, living out their lives only to see to it that others should be able to enjoy the good life. Yet, the power of self-deception is so great that in spite of the patent nonsense of these claims, one can hardly doubt that most who make this claim of selfless devotion to the welfare of others mean it with some degree of sincerity.

A predictable feature of such benevolent paternalistic relations is the frequent failure of the powerless to show a "proper amount" of gratitude and appreciation—a failure that tends to be resented deeply by the powerful. For the failure to appreciate the altruism of motives denies the prepotence of altruism in the whole complex of motives that engage the powerful, and lays bare the other self-serving motives that are simultaneously present in that complex.

This is why despairing parents finally learn that a full appreciation of what they have done for their children cannot be expected, if ever, until those children in turn receive the full impact and brunt of the ingratitude of their children.

The most sophisticated version of the new benevolent paternalism is that mode (found most prominently among the most hip of parents and the most permissive of psychiatrists) which insists on sharing power with children or patients, on the grounds that the child-patient has to make his own mistakes. In one fell swoop, thereby, obeisance is paid to freedom and equality, while confidence is retained in the power of the true theory and of greater experience. For this freedom is granted on the assumption that the experiences had during that freedom will be valid and useful only in so far as they bring home forcefully to the child the realization of how mistaken he was in his decisions. No concession is made to the possibility that the child may grow more effectively by the experiences he chooses, however mistaken these experiences may be in the eyes of the parent or psychiatrist, than if he had pursued the true path chosen for him at the time. It is no accident, then, that the philosophy of existentialism, the cult of experience, and a systematic indifference to future consequences should have come so amply to characterize the orientations of so many of the youth today.

There is a twofold danger in this pseudo-permissiveness. First, freedom is contagious and self-commending—almost as much as security and protection—so that once experienced it is not likely to be surrendered easily. Certainly it cannot easily be recalled on demand by the original donor. Second, life's experiences are such that most often one cannot easily prove that a given year would have had a better net result if a hypothetical alternative course had been pursued rather than the one actually followed. So the benevolent parent or psychiatrist can't really prove his point in the long run, especially if, as also often happens, some pride and defensiveness characterize the child or patient in his new willfullness. Moreover, the parent or psychiatrist cannot ever give as much value-weight to the sheer exhilaration of freedom as the child or patient must unavoidably ascribe to that experience. Thus, each participant can look back on the earlier parting of the ways, and evaluate the consequences of the freedom in starkly different terms. Only the best novelists manage to tell all of us how these different definitions of the situation emerge, what they mean to each party concerned, and in what ways they corrosively widen the gap in possible sharing and intimacy for the future.

Perhaps by now enough has been said to justify the claim that the way in which power is distributed in a relationship is a crucial determinant of conduct, and that inequality in power is characteristic most of the time of most relationships, from the most intimate interpersonal level to that of the largest social aggregates.

On this assumption it becomes pertinent to suggest that the metaphor of captor and captive is fitting in some ways to characterize social relationships marked by an imbalance of power among the participants. It is no accident that the characteristics that mark so-called *total institutions* (such as prisons, ships, and concentration camps) can be applied with appropriate modifications to the range of the most usual and frequent relationships in which we all engage—families, schools, churches, offices and plants, hospitals, doctors' offices, social work agencies, and international organizations.

To speak in terms of captor and captive is especially useful in an age and a culture where the terms *consent* and *consensus* are bandied about freely and where it is thereby implied that the conduct of affairs, personal and public, is at bottom a matter of discussion, compromise, and agreement among equally endowed and equally powerful participants. Nothing could be less appropriate, however, than to speak of consent and consensus when the power to *dissent* with impunity is unequally distributed. For the ability to agree and to compromise presumes the ability *not* to agree without suffering unequal loss. And unequal power insures that this ability *not* to agree will be unequally available. In many of the relationships in which today's elite moralize about the importance of consent, the other party's consent is about as free as when they contract to pay a high rate of interest on a loan which they desperately need and cannot elsewhere secure.

The captor-captive metaphor is valuable, too, because it helps reveal the unreality of the insistence by the disproportionately powerful that all members of the society, however powerless, should take equal responsibility onto their shoulders for the conduct of society. Again, the assumption of responsibility presupposes the power necessary to discharge that responsibility, and the correlative power to avoid or create certain lines of policy and consequence. Minus such power, it is meaningless and false to urge that responsibility should be equally shared.

The prevalence in centers of power of the doctrines of consensus and of equal responsibility in the circles of official spokesmen of established institutions is totally expectable. For if the real power to command lies unequally with them, then it is clearly to their decided advantage to advocate consensus, when in effect this will mean the promulgations of policies that are far more in accordance with their interests than with those held by the less powerful. The same considerations apply to the moral issues of obligation, credit and blame for the conduct of social affairs. One is very fortunate if, while retaining a preponderance of power, he manages to get acceptance of the notion that moral obligations should be equal.

The metaphor of *captor-and-captive* in social relationships is often far more apt and fitting to the actual conditions than *partner*. It serves the function of reminding us to whom we shall turn when seeking the agents responsible for the state of affairs. Perhaps too, the intrusion of the captor-captive metaphor will contribute toward the continuing challenge to existing distributions of power, so that in the long run the equality of power necessary for equality of responsibility may be more closely approximated.

We are impelled by these distinctions to suggest the further importance of distinguishing three different ways in which norms can be followed and apparent social harmony achieved. The distinction rests chiefly on three different degrees of equality in the distribution of power and other resources required for genuinely equal participation in decision making.

We may speak first of *compliance* as the condition under which people do as they are asked or expected to do, either because they do not know of alternatives, or they feel powerless to disobey, or some combination of both. Where, however, there is at least some knowledge of alternatives, and some power to say no, and some possibility of personal gain, however little in proportion to responsibility and effort, we may then speak of *conformity*. Third, under the condition that a range of alternatives are known and present, and that the concerned parties have resources with which to decide among them and to choose those that in their judgment will maximize their welfare, given all the relevant values and limits, under these conditions we may speak of *consent* or consensus.

In any given instance then, the decision as to whether *compliance, conformity,* or *consent* are the proper terms to apply depends on the degrees of effective freedom to choose and to implement alternatives that are available to the participants. Social harmony can be found under any of the three conditions, in the sense that peace, order, and stability can characterize the social structure. But it obviously makes all the difference in the world, so far as human lives are concerned, how that harmony is achieved. We should be very short of the mark if we were not to recognize that conflict may be unmistakably preferable to peace and harmony under some conditions, and that in any event, no decision can be made *a priori* regarding the general or normal preferability of conflict to stability or vice versa.

It can now be asserted that throughout the world, and at every level of social interaction, a revolutionary struggle is taking place to eliminate the conditions that generate compliance and conformity and to foster those that make genuine consent possible. Everywhere former underdogs are pushing for new powers in their traditional relationships with topdogs. Women versus men, children versus adults, pupils versus teachers, teachers versus principals, Negroes versus Whites, poor versus rich, criminals versus the police, wives versus husbands, clients and patients versus lawyers and doctors and architects and social workers; these are but some of the more permanent relationships in which the new demands for greater equality are being made.

In response, the traditionally powerful seek to retain their privileged positions, for the voluntary surrender of power and privilege, without other compensating gains, is a rare event in human affairs. While whatever changes that do take place must be seen as dominantly due to the pressures exerted by the under-privileged partners in these relationships, it must be admitted that the underdogs are curiously often aided and abetted by the more conscientious among the privileged elite—who sometimes help draft new laws and norms, and help disseminate (out of

ideology *cum* guilt) general cultural encouragement toward greater
equality.

Unavoidably, as the pressures toward change mount, and as the
atmosphere favorable to it increases, the privileged groups find that
the underdogs are asking for too much too soon. As a result, the
abstract enthusiasm of the privileged for the new liberties and
equalities to be accorded the underdogs begins rapidly and con-
cretely to dampen. On the other side, some of the underprivileged
who have waited so long for such moments, see no good reason now
to be cautious or reserved about the new powers they seek and the
new roles they demand to be allowed to play. A new set of conflicts are thus put in motion. The counterreactive cautions of the
elite are met and matched by the increased militance of the under-
privileged. Sometimes the former positions are partly reversed, so
that the new powerful are able, within certain limits, to command
a degree of compliance, albeit a most reluctant form, from their
captors.

Examples of these reactions and counterreactions on the modern
scene come readily to mind, especially from the arenas of combat
between Negroes and Whites and parents and children. Several
important principles govern these reactions, principles that must
be understood if participants and spectators are not to be dismayed
and overwhelmed by the turns of events. There is, first, the principle
of *inverse reciprocity*. On this principle, the so-called benefactors
in any relationship are those who are most often and most severely
condemned and punished by those whom they supposedly aided.
This condemnation and punishment start the moment the captives
get the courage, strength and energy to speak and act for themselves,
namely, the moment they develop the kind of self-help orientation
that their democratic benefactors have presumably been working
hard to help them acquire. The dynamics here are complex, but
some of the mechanisms at work can now be distinguished. Most significant is the fact that the benefactors have been privileged and
intimate witnesses to the degradation of the captives. They are
the people who knew the captives "when"; as such, the benefactors
are intolerable. The new power and status of the captives would
lose much of its significance for them if they had to admit, by
indulging in gratitude to those who helped them, that they could

not have "made it" without the aid of the benefactors. Thus, inverse reciprocity is required—almost absolutely—if the doctrine of self-help is to receive any real implementation. Knowing how this mechanism operates, benefactors (or captors) must be fully prepared for it; they must somehow find a way in which to be joyous about its operations, since they are the mark of the emergence of the self out of captivity and helplessness, and presumably this is what benefactors (not captors) have really and earnestly wanted all along. Of great significance in these changing situations is the fact that the new distribution of power also results in a new distribution of social and personal *fear*, so that now Whites come to fear Negroes more than ever before, husbands fear wives, parents fear children, teachers fear students, and the most powerful nations unavoidably have to act out of fear of new and relatively powerless nations.

We have, I believe, a good deal to learn from analyzing the sources of these new fears, most particularly those relevant to the relations between Negroes and Whites, which have been symbolized most dramatically in the demands for "Black Power." For there is no good reason why Whites should have come to fear Negroes in view of the fact that beyond question the clearly dominant power still lies in the hands of the Whites. But now we can see that the demand by Negroes for power is fearful precisely because most Whites have never thought of themselves as an identifiable group— a white collectivity exercising power over a Negro collectivity. Rather, they have tended to consider themselves individually (or at best their families or small neighborhoods), as relatively tiny and isolated units, relatively powerless to face and resist the apparent collective upsurge of the whole Negro group. Whites in short almost never form a self-conscious collectivity, something purposefully organized to maintain and control the relationships with Negroes, however much impersonally their collective actions in fact add up to such a collective force, and however much the Negro group has contrariwise tended to see all Whites as united in their restraint of Negro rights and freedoms.

The same observations apply to the relations between parents and children, or adults and youth. The new demands for power seem to emanate from an entire generation or cohort, but seem also to be focused alone on each of us individually, with our own children or youth acting not as individuals in relation to us as individuals, but as representatives of an entire generation and backed to some menacing extent by its collective force and strength.

This apparently collective attack upon us as individuals, as we perceive it, is all the more threatening and dismaying because in some senses most of us have good reasons to feel powerless in general, however much we may sense and exercise our powers in the limited context of our families. We are here implying an important distinction between diverse loci of power in human relationships. One must distinguish, we believe, *role power*, or the ability to direct a particular relationship, on the one hand, from *personal power*, or the ability to shape one's general life scheme according to his wishes—including the range of the diverse roles the one plays on the other. Finally, there is *social power*, or the ability to influence the course of events of social groups or collectivities of which we are members, whether they be the formal bureaucracies in which we work or fight or teach or pray, or the local state or national communities of which we are citizens.

Some of us, if we are lucky, have some limited power in one or two of our major roles, usually family and work. But only the rarest of us has any good reason to feel the least bit powerful with regard to the totality of his personal life, and even less reason to act as if he were influential with regard to the directions taken by the other collectivities of which he is a member or a citizen. And even the power that some of us are able to exert within specific role relationships is almost always hedged and restricted or balanced out, since—especially in bureaucratic structures—there is almost always someone (if not many) who are powerful over us, however much we may have our own subordinates.

It thus ends up that out of the totality of situations relevant to our lives, we are powerful, if at all, in only a very small minority of cases, and the ends we can thereby achieve are relatively miniscule compared to those over whose achievements we have little control. Small wonder then that the tendency is ubiquitous to overexercise such few powers as we do have, to the usual dismay and discontent of the captives in these relationships, who quite justifiably, from their point of view, find us unreasonably arrogant, totalitarian and unfair. Little wonder, too, that when these few, often pitiful bastions of role or personal power are challenged, we should feel so basically fearful and threatened, when, objectively, they represent a very small portion of the totality of life's ends with which we are concerned. For if we lose our power in these few areas of life, what then will remain to us?

We are today at some such condition of life in most of our social relationships, whether interpersonal, intergroup, or international. And however much the underprivileged may relish the new equalization of fear, and seek to capitalize on it, and however much abstractly and from a safe distance some few of the traditional elite may applaud the partial turning of the tables, it cannot long be denied that this is altogether a nasty state of affairs, and one out of which a democratic society and sane people had best seek the quickest possible release.

In which directions then are we likely to go? And toward what ends should we be seeking to go? An abundance of evidence argues strongly that the only viable direction for a democratic society and for a sane people—and perhaps the only possible direction short of catastrophe—is toward a new equilibrium in which ever greater equality of privilege and power are the characteristic features. The only alternative possibility—reinstating even more repressive captor-captive relationships—is an obvious social nightmare. However much some may dream of the desirability of the return to such earlier conditions, the institutional and ideological bases for such counter-reformations are now no longer present. This is not to say that a pervasive and massive totalitarianization of relationships could not take place under the right circumstances, but it is to insist that it is precisely that kind of totalitarianization and all its concomitants that represent the only alternatives to greater equality and freedom in human relationships.

In part, therefore, the direction of probable change is also the direction of desirable change, given certain democratic value preferences. But it may be useful to indicate some other good grounds on which to move as quickly and as resolutely as possible toward that new equality and toward those new social roles. If these grounds are kept firmly in mind, they may enable the timid among us—that is virtually all of us—to habituate ourselves more quickly to the new ideas, the new sharing, the new kinds of social partnerships that must emerge out of the captor-captive relationships that have heretofore been dominant. For if on the one hand we have a deeply lodged set of old vested interests (preserving our existing privileges and powers), we have on the other hand an equally salient set of new vested interests (learning how to share these privileges)—how to live in the new world that such sharing will necessarily create.

Among those other good reasons, there stands out first the fact that given the impetus for change that is now operating, any serious effort to resist these changes is sure to generate bitter interpersonal and social conflict beyond anything that most us have experienced short of the World Wars. Moreover, if we resist and are nominally successful, we shall not simply be preserving the status quo. Rather we shall have instituted a new form of captivity, in which the captives are immensely more restive, discontent, and ready to engage in conflict than ever before. For now the die is cast; the alternatives are known, the new possibilities are evident, and the ideological defenses of the captor-captive relationships are no longer serviceable. Any effort to retain old powers must now be justified, if at all, only on the admittedly morally indefensible grounds that might makes right. The former compliance based on ignorance and fear, and the former conformity based on apathy and fear, will no longer be available. A new conformity, characterized by hostility, sullen discontent and alert readiness to rebel and deviate will come to prevail.

A second good reason to be active in implementation of new equalities and freedoms is the fact that most of our old relationships simply don't work well—not even for those in command. Every formal power scheme, whether in a family, a prison, factory, army, state or public school, generates informal subcultures of discontent and subversion, such that, in at least some of the cases, the dominant captors are prevented, by the very institutionalization of their powers, from achieving the ends they seek.

For example, prisons simply do not reform. At best they maintain a status quo. More usually, they act as schools for crime and graduate more skillful criminals at that.

So, too, in some significant senses, family structures no longer serve the ends intended by the members, including exchange of affection and acceptance, without regard to competitive achievement in the external world. There is good reason to suppose that there is ever mounting discontent between spouses and among parents and children. Our verbal invitations to freedom and our casual ideological defenses of independence for children are chronically dissonant with our actions. Our hypocrisies become more evident and painful to all concerned. Our wives are captured by the dilemma between house and world, our husbands by their jobs, and our children by their peers—perhaps more than ever before in our social history. We live often in ignorance of what effects we are having on our children, and with a growing sense of impotence both with regard to providing them the help we feel they need or in securing the love and respect we want from them. Let the more blessed among us, who do not recognize this as a fair description of their realities, be generous in their silence while in the company of the less blessed among us for whom this captures at least some of the actuality of our lives.

Another instance of self-subverting unequal power is the public school system, which while performing marvelous and prodigious feats in some sectors, fails miserably in others. Writing of the culture of the schools, and with special reference to the role of teachers, Seymour Sarason has noted that "Innovations or changes practically never reflect the initiative of teachers but rather the highest levels of administration. Those who initiate change generally adopt means which maximize the strengths of the reactions which can only dilute or subvert the intent of the innovations.... [Partly this is due to the fact] that from the standpoint of teachers, they are the most frequent and convenient objects of criticism, from within as well as without the system, in regard to policies and programs which were not of their making."

So too in industry. Dozens of sociologists have made their reputations in the last two decades documenting the numerous ways in which the structures of bureaucracy that are set up presumably in response to the demands for efficiency help generate subversive counterstructures among the workers, among whose principal gratifications is the reduction of productivity. In some important sense, of course, the emergence of trade unions, and their unavoidable need to pose worker interests against those of management, is a direct responsibility of the unequal power of management.

A number of scholars have also shown us how these subversive counterstructures arise in the adolescent society. David Matza and Albert Cohen have documented this brilliantly for the world of those juveniles who have run against the normative order. August Hollingshead, James Coleman, and others have produced substantial evidence of peer group cultures that operate directly at cross purposes with those of the school and of the parent community.

Here, too, the evidence from studies of hospital structure and functioning, especially mental hospitals, is cogent and salient. Stanton and Schwartz, among others, have shown how patient subcultures, generated in the interstices of power that any bureaucracy necessarily leaves unoccupied, come often to subvert the therapeutic milieu.

We are all only too familiar, as well, with the extent and frequency with which social welfare relationships between specialist and client have degenerated so that deception and fraud become characteristic themes. What else should we expect in the cultural atmosphere where the quick buck is the smartest and best buck, where systematic evasion of the tax law by the wealthy is paraded as endemic, and where acceptance of the traditional role of grateful recipient of welfare dubs one as helpless, hapless, degraded and despised?

Further examples and illustrations do not have to be multiplied here. The data is well known to all professionals in the field. The conclusion one can draw from this data is that a prominent source of difficulty in achieving the stated ends of any social enterprise or institution is the unequal distribution of power in these relationships.

The sequence of events can easily be traced. Unequal power means unequal profit from the enterprise, unequal honor for its conduct, and unequal capacity to identify with the enterprise. These in turn lead to unequal belief in and commitment to the desirability of the goals and of the means used to achieve those goals. Such unequal commitment, in turn, leads to one of several different directions of action, all of them to some degree disfunctional for the social enterprise. The least conflictive path is characterized by apathy and withdrawal, with consequent lowering of morale, motivation, and productivity. A more conflictive form involves quasi-active hostility and resentment, including as well partial rejection both of the goals and the means. The most difficult reaction, from the point of view of the captor society, involves active rejection of the goals or means or both, and the substitution of deviant forms of behavior, both of ends and means, in direct and active opposition to existing norms.

The personal and social losses arising from these reactions to unequal power and hence unequal identification with the conduct of a relationship are also matters of record. We can calculate only too well the loss of manpower, productivity, and personal and social wealth and well-being that result, for instance, from the systematic discrimination against the Negro. The lowered efficiency of industrial organizations is also a source of chronic complaint. The failure of families is endemic. The increased distance between adults and youth is by now a banal albeit ever-distressful tale of woe.

These then are some of the other good reasons why it is imperative that a democratic society and a sane people should explore the possibilities contained in the construction of new roles in basic social relationships. This is not to argue that more equal power is the panacea for all social and personal woes. Relationships fail for more reasons than can be encompassed by the terms of power alone. But the contribution of inequality in power and identification to those failures is unquestionable.

From a neutral social science point of view, there is much to be learned and gained from analyzing the dialectic of these relationships, for a number of important sociological principles are illustrated and clarified by them.

There is first the principle of *cumulative relative deprivation*. This refers to the process by which discontent with status and condition increase in direct proportion to the improvement of status and condition. In vulgar, understandable terms, the better off one gets, the worse off one feels. For persons with long life histories of captivity and deprivation, this development is totally natural, simply because it takes the emergence of a horizon of possibility to energize even a minimum level of active discontent. Life cannot be seen as bad, until some possibility of it being much better is in sight, and until this possibility is seen as one within the reach of the aspirant. Therefore, we must expect that the answer to the question, "What do they want," will be "Everything"; and the response to the query, "When will they be satisfied," is "Never."

Of such stuff, indeed, are made the Protestant ethic, the need for achievement, and the struggle for maximizing potentialities—all three being the essence of theories of personal and social development which captor classes develop with great skill at the moments of their greatest preponderance of power.

An equally important sociological principle in operation here may be termed that of "capital deformation." By contrast with the economic fantasy called "capital formation," this process operates so that any and all gains acquired in the process of emerging from captivity are consumed before they can be invested for long-range construction, whether social, psychic or economic. The captor groups or echelons are thus required to contribute more and more of their own hoarded resources to get the captives past a so-called take-off point. (In some quarters today this draining of captor resources is justified under the terms of the principle of "historical compensation.") The limit of captor patience in this process is reached with notorious speed. But captor patience has little to do with how long capital deformation continues. The benefactor group must learn somehow to temper its acerbic impatience and sense of increased deprivation with the realization that if it truly desires the former victims to reach the take-off point, it had better be prepared to pay rather large compensatory prices, however difficult it is to pay off now and almost all at once for moral debts acquired over a long period of time.

So, too, perhaps the temptation of the benefactor echelon to lash back at the ever increasing demands of the formerly-captive group may be somewhat mitigated if they realize and accept the fact that though the captives are behaving in the so-called irresponsible fashion typical of the least moral member of any group, the morality at stake is after all that of the benefactors, and it is their collective historical participation in the deprivation of the captives which converted them into the least moral participants.

In turn, the captives, emerging into new power, must themselves come to awareness of the operations of the principle of the *most proximate pecker*—that is, to realize that the most serious status clashes occur between the newly arisen group and those closest to them in the status-pecking order. For the emergence of the captives most threatens serious status deprivation for those most proximate to them.

Now, among those who perceive the probable unavoidability of these changes and affirm the desirability of change in the abstract, there are a growing number who are most cautious about the concrete desirability of these changes on the grounds that the *nouveaux puissants* will be inept, untutored, unskillful, clumsy, and will only make things worse for everyone—including themselves—if they are given more effective roles in the management of their own affairs. However accurate some of these predictions may be, they must be seen first as within the genre of reactions whose classic model is the reaction of the aristocracy to the idea of greater participation by the *nouveaux riches* in enterprises where taste and sensibility were at stake. The prediction then was (and now is) that the new rich will be vulgar, banal, sentimental and tawdry in their choices, thereby destroying all the fine things which the old rich had presumably created and which, unfortunately, could only be enjoyed properly by them.

As always in such matters, there is a question of competing sets of values. One may admire and respect the refinement and delicacy in tastes and sensibilities of the privileged elite. But one has to wonder how much they are worth if the total value context in which they have traditionally flourished has involved the degradation, exploitation and barbarization of the lives of the many.

So too with the sharing of power. One may confidently expect outlandish inefficiencies, misuses of funds, new kinds of nepotisms, temporary, if not enduring, losses in many desired values and outcomes. But this is to see the matter primarily from the point of view of those things most cherished by the privileged groups.

And how much, then, are these to be weighed in the balance against the chance that by developing new roles through the sharing of power, we may be creating the conditions necessary for the emergence of a new kind of civilization in which apathy, anomie, helplessness, and degradation are not the fate and fortunes of the many? Or, in which the systematic ruination of the morals and morality of our children will not be the predictable outcome of our excesses of indulgence and of severity, generated by our guilts and fears? Or in which boredom and ennui will not be the dominant tone of marital relationships once the first flushes of romantic love and youthful sexual desire have burnt themselves out? Or in which the dominant level of thinking about the responsibilities of the mass media is not characterized by the patently self-serving and culturally destructive notion that the masses get what they want, or at least what they deserve. Or in which schools may be conducted in such a way that something more than College Board scores on verbal and mathematical abilities are the measures of their achievement and admissions to prestigious Ivy League Colleges the guarantees of their success.

These are not utopian ideas, though it would not matter much if they were. They represent the real chances we have in this world. We are systematically kept from moving toward them by the unequal distribution of power, which generates the subsequent lack of self-respect and of respect by others and the concomitant lack of concern about and active participation in the affairs of our society.

Finally, even if all the dire predictions about what will happen if power were to be shared were realized, it seems unavoidable to conclude that it is the moral obligation of a democratic society to move ahead toward that end. If that is the obligation, and if, in some important senses it is also unavoidable, it would be the better part of wisdom and sensibility to accede to the new demands with some degree of graciousness and to help them come into being.

Every other adult generation has gone down in the face of changes that overwhelmed its norms, fighting, complaining and bitter. Perhaps it will be possible to give evidence that culture and wisdom do cumulate, if today's custodians of power prepare to exit from their privileged posts with a graciousness that other generations have not been able to muster or exhibit. To be gracious in defeat is as signal a token of civilization as to be generous in victory. And, in the last analysis, by cooperating in our particular defeat, we also share in our general victory.

COMMENTARY

EUGEN PUSIĆ

My first reaction, after having read a few pages of Professor Tumin's paper, was to become confused about the time in the century: "Is it 1984 already? I thought we were only in 1966." But as I continued to read what appeared at first as one of the blackest utopias I have come across, the ideas seemed to me more and more like those I should have held or expressed myself had I been doing my work properly and not running around the world. Here was one instance of somebody getting ahead of me in what I have always considered to be my own original line of thought. I re-read Professor Tumin's paper carefully and the impression persisted. The atmosphere of pessimism as well as the feeling of familiarity and the nearness of conviction were close to my thoughts.

This feeling of *déja vue* occurs in fields less vague than those of the social sciences. Some ideas are "in the air" at a certain moment in time and, consequently, people coming from widely different starting points reach startlingly similar conclusions. Is it possible, then, that I have not drawn the necessary pessimistic inferences from my own conclusions, which seem to me to run parallel to those of Professor Tumin? I will simply try to think out loud in an "agonizing reappraisal."

"Power," as we all know, is a tricky word. The problem starts with linguistics. In English "power" has a confusing wide connotation, so that Locke, for instance, could speak of the power of the wax to be melted by heat. In the Slavic languages, for example, we have two different expressions for power as a social relationship (particularly for political power) and for power as a possibility of achieving an effect. But more than problems of language is implied in Professor Tumin's definition. Professor Tumin speaks of "the power of the true theory." In that sense, the power of the objective situation in the outside world to limit our intentions and activities seems to me essentially different from the use of "power" to denote the possibility of human action in a social relationship against human opposition. I think that Professor Tumin has in mind only this last mentioned, more restricted understanding of "power." But the ambiguity is there.

The ambiguity explains, perhaps, the pervasiveness of power in human relations that he assumes and it creates the impression of fatalism conveyed to me by the first part of his paper. Power is there, always, and if it does not show it is because it is held back by the powerful for purposes of their own to further some other power-goal. There is a danger in such a theory of "power" becoming a concept similar to that of "challenge" in the work of Toynbee, a concept which, by definition, cannot be operationalized, detected, measured or in any other way proved or disproved. If it is there, we see it. If it is not, we assume it has been checked, or covered even if it is still there.

The main question is whether we regard power as a primary element of human behavior—as something which needs no further cause or explanation, a primordial drive which is simply here and has to be explained only in terms of the various forms in which it is manifested. An affirmative answer to this question seems possible to me but far from self-evident; if there is any systematic empirical evidence, it has escaped my knowledge.

On the contrary, most of the literature on the various concrete forms of power (economic, political, etc.) seems to assume the instrumental character of power. These works see power as a means of achieving field-specific aims, such as the accumulation of capital, the expansion of production, the implementation of political programs, the changing of the existing socio-economic structure, etc.

For our discussion, ultimately, it does not make a great difference which of the two points of view we assume, whether we consider power as a basic instinct or as an instrument. If we are to discuss the phenomenon at all we must assume, even in the first alternative, that the forms of the manifestation of power change so significantly that the social role of power and the whole social situation determined by it is affected. Then, of course, we have to explain the causes of these changes, and that leaves us with practically the same problems as if we had assumed the secondary, instrumental point of view on power in the first place.

One important difference, however, becomes evident. The instrumental hypothesis seems to me to be much more fruitful as an approach to explaining the visible changes in the social role of power, because I think that we are not simply interested in a situation where somebody gets a chance to realize his intentions against the opposition of somebody else. We are interested however, in the situation where chance persists over a period of time wherein an individual (or a group of individuals) can impose his will on others systematically, continuously, relatively smoothly, i.e., without each single instance being an issue which has to be fought out. These are also the examples which Professor Tumin mentions.

Such forms of systematic, persisting power-situations seem to require the fulfillment of two preconditions (beside the actual possibility of imposing one's will) for overcoming opposition. They presuppose a motivation in the power-holders for the constant exercise of power over others, and an inducement for those over whom power is exercised to be continuously submissive to it.

Really, we cannot avoid the question of motivation by assuming an ubiquitous instinct for power in man. This only shifts the need of explanation to the question of why some power-relationships are relatively constant over a period of time, while others are not. Initially, it seems simpler to assume that the exercise of power is motivated by the wish to protect or implement an interest of the power-holders. In economics, when the total production in a community is not large enough to satisfy the material interests of all its members the problem arises as to who will get the larger share. It is precisely this situation which transforms a class of objects into a commodity—something which is not simply used but appropriated, distributed, exchanged, sold, bought. Power might be used to influence systematically the outcome of instances of competition for scarce goods in favor of one individual or group of individuals against others. Political power and its use might sometimes be explained by economic interests as well, but certainly not always. There are a great number of other possible interests. Let us think, for instance, of the categories established by Hans Zetterberg in his *Social Theory and Social Practice*. And power can be used to achieve systematic domination of one class of interests over another in a widely varying set of interest conflicts. These interests, however, should not simply be assumed when we come across a socially significant persisting power-relationship. The relationship should be questioned, investigated, analyzed.

The knowledge of the underlying interest and its probable trend in the future is one of the essential conditions for attempting a prognosis as to the possible development and change of power relationships. The other is an understanding of the acceptance of domination by the dominated.

The classic position of Max Weber on this question is that

people obey because they simply do not question long-established tradition, because they are fascinated by the charismatic appeal of a personality or an idea, or because they accept a legally established power as being in accord with "the rules of the game," believing at the same time in the necessity of rules. Though this classification applies, in the intentions of its author, only to political power, to "Herrschaft," it is a good occasion to discuss the question of the interest-position of the ruled. Charismatic and legal power, by their definitions, do not imply the use of direct physical force in their establishment or maintenance, and traditional power relegates it to a dimly visible past. In any case, what has been said concerning political power is even more true of other power relationships. You can do anything with bayonets except sit on them.

In the majority of cases, it is hardly conceivable that relationships of domination would persist for long centuries without a compensating "pay-off" to the dominated; captives—very often representing a numerical majority—would not rebel and throw off their captors if they did not see any profit whatsoever from the relationship in which they play the role of the underdog. I submit, for instance, that the power of parents begins to wane at the moment when it is no longer based on the usefulness of their greater experience and greater proficiency in supporting the children who are subject to their power; similarly, the power of the owners of the means of production is based on their role as entrepreneurs and creators of job opportunities; and in the same way, the power of governments is based on their maintenance of the public order and the provision of public services. I think that this conclusion is not disproved by the fact that in a moment of crisis the power-holders do lean heavily on organized physical violence and constraint to maintain their position. What we need to explain is how they come to possess the means to exercise this physical force sometimes over a long period of time.

It follows that a socially significant persisting power-relationship can be maintained only if—and as long as—there exists a sufficiently compelling motive on the part of the power-holders, and a convincing enough inducement for those subject to power, to enforce the responsibility to mutually accept an asymmetric situation as the only possibility of satisfying their separate interests.

In starting from these premises, it appears to me—and here basically I agree with Professor Tumin—that we are witnessing a very important change in the motivation and the inducement factors supporting the historically developed power-relationships, at least some of them. These changes are related to the role of hierarchy in the coordination of men at work, to the role of governments in providing order and service, and to the role of scarcity in creating interest-conflicts.

The expectations of a managerial revolution and of the emergence of a totally organized society both with their dark implications are based on the assumption that organization necessarily means hierarchy, a relationship of subordination and superordination, and therefore, a relationship of domination by power. Let us examine this assumption from the point of view of motivation and of legitimation.

The work in a factory, a shop, and from there transposed to any organization, has been developed, since the Industrial Revolution, on the principle of dividing a complex task into progressively smaller and simpler components, by fracturing the total work process into quite simple operations. The final outcome of this development is the industrial conveyor belt where people of comparatively low skill can perform very complex tasks by having assigned to them a small and simple part of the full job, the parts being brought into relationship with each other in such a way that the final result is the accomplishment of the total task. In the course of this development, a continuous power-relationship has been established going from the top to the bottom of the described process of division of work, which is called hierarchy. The motivation for the maintenance of this relationship on the part of the upper echelons of the hierarchy is their relatively favorable position in the acquisition of benefits derived from the work process; the inducement for the lower strata is the possibility to participate, with some profit for themselves, in a process which would otherwise be beyond their level of skill and ability. The basic rationale for the whole relationship, however, is that hierarchy expresses approximately correctly the objective needs of the work-process and the objective existing relationship of skill and ability among the participants. When it ceases to do so, the basis of its existence and its acceptance are undermined.

In my opinion, that is what is happening today. On the one hand, the proportion of high-level specialists working in organizations is increasing. On the other hand, human participation in routine operations has been transformed by the advent of automation. If a task can be simplified by breaking it up into elementary components, these components can be transferred to machines. The specialists, on the other hand, do not perform routine operations. As a rule, their work-process remains intact. It is only specialized in the sense of being related to a narrower segment of the total situation which confronts us. In this narrower sector, however, the specialist is doing a whole job, involving judgment and a creative attitude towards his task. This new relationship makes hierarchy unnecessary and unacceptable—unnecessary because the work is not divided any more in a way that requires progressively lower skills and simpler operations as you go "down the line"; unacceptable because the cooperation of highly skilled specialists can be achieved much better on the principle of the team (the work-group-of-equals) than by hierarchical command.

At the same time this change is taking place in business and industry, comparable change is occurring in the role of governments. The public sector no longer has to be identified with government, with political power. It is probable that the provision of public services will grow in the future. But even today many of these services are provided by independent agencies (whose ties with political power are rather nominal), or even by international agencies who have no backing by the organized instruments of compulsion of any state. Their functional aim and purpose seem to be enough to provide them with the necessary orientation. Governments also have had their "balance of usefulness" shifted by the increasing danger from an armed conflict among sovereign states. Even admitting some positive contribution by governments to the performance of socially necessary functions, the total gain has to be compared with the increased risk from conflicts. It is becoming evident that these conflicts have really nothing to do with the interests of the peoples the governments purport to represent, but are international power clashes among competing organizations whose traditional main purpose is none other than to produce superior instruments of systematic violence. Even if the motivation of the political power-holders persists, the inducement for their subjects—which has consisted of the security and services only political power could, supposedly, provide—is certainly disappearing.

Generally speaking, however, one of the most important motivations for maintaining relations of domination by power, the scarcity of material goods, tends to be significantly modified. There is no question about it. Technically, and in the foreseeable future, we can be in a position to produce a sufficient amount of goods to satisfy the basic material needs of all people on earth.

The relative improvement of a group's position by the possibility of satisfying its material needs, however, has certainly been one of the most abundant sources of interest-conflict in the past. Should the importance of this source decrease in the future—and the technical preconditions of such a decrease are given—it seems reasonable to expect that this will influence significantly the motivation for the establishment of power-relationships calculated to achieve economic interest domination.

All these factors contribute to the conclusion that we are on the threshold of very important developments, or rather possibilities of developments. For here enters into the picture the secondary persistence of power relationships beyond their instrumental purpose. Hardened by habit, obstructing the view of new factors, reinforced by appropriate ideologies, value systems, etc., existing power institutions tend to be defended beyond the point of diminishing returns. But not indefinitely beyond this point. We do not have an indefinite time before us to wait. It is really a race against the growing dangers from power and power-conflicts which makes our situation problematical and increases our responsibility for action.

COMMENTARY

LUCIEN MEHL

It is a very difficult task indeed to comment on this exceptionally interesting paper which is so expectedly full of new ideas, because the participants to the Colloquium were invited to discuss, if not initiate, "social inventions."

But my duty as a commentator is to contest and argue—in a

friendly way—for the sake of liveliness of the Colloquium. "L'ennui naquit un jour de l'uniformité," and I suppose that uniformity of opinions is particularly irrelevant in a discussion group. I shall also try to remain conscious of my relative ignorance in sociology. But I hope that my juridical training will help me to find arguments for the discussion.

It seems to me that the fundamental and original idea of Professor Tumin's paper resides in the coupled concept of "captor and captive," especially if it is considered in its relation to the notion of power (individual and social).

I. Philosophical Interest of the Dipole Captor-Captive

The philosophical interest of this concept is probably due to its generality, not only in the social field, but also in metaphysics. It is a key to the comprehension of the human condition.

In his relation to his natural environment, physical or biological, man is simultaneously or successively captor and captive. In order to become master and regulator of his milieu, he must obey its laws: "Naturae non imperatur nisi parendo." The same for time. We are the prey of time, but we try to remember the past, to seize the present while it is action, and to organize the future by our projects. When we hear music, we are, at the same moment, the captive and the captor of time; perhaps this is the reason for the emotional character of music.

More generally, due to the conflicts inside of ourselves between spirit and body, reason and instinct, "Ueber-ich" and inconscient ego, we are alternatively captor and captive of our own being.

In the religious feeling, the dualism, captor-captive is quite obvious, especially in the "revealed" religions which affirm the existence of a personal god, omniscient and omnipotent.

Then man may appear to be captive: the problem of the conciliation between human liberty, divine grace and predestination is a subject for subtle and passionate controversies.

But this conciliation is considered to be quite impossible by certain philosophical schools and especially by the atheistic existentialists.

If such a personal god exists, Jean-Paul Sartre says, then man is nothing. But Sartre denies the existence of God. The man is alone, but man is all and man is free and he has to define and control his destiny.

Of course in this "Weltanschauung," as in the Christian conception, the human condition is considered to be dreadful and miserable. But this condition of mankind is more acceptable since the world is not described as being the work of a learned and powerful god.

Man can accept death, disease, sufferings, and all the absurdities of his condition if the universe, especially humanity and society are self-creating and self-evolving through a long, painstaking and uncertain process. It is possible to forgive the world its contradictions and failures, because "natura naturans" does not oblige me to "love" it and cooperate. I may say "yes" or "no," without incurring any transcendental judgment. Then I am free, because I have the power to dissent. Nobody can compel me to act by making reference "to needs and wishes of a non-empirically verifiable entity." If I decide to cooperate for a better world and society, it is a free decision. Of course, as I have said, I am a captive of nature, but I also capture it. The relation is reciprocal and so the game is equitable.

II. Power, Equality and Liberty in the Society

Now if we consider the social field, we see Professor Tumin has clearly shown that the dipole "captor-captive" is also very general. The distribution of individual potentialities and of social authority is fundamentally unequal. I agree with Professor Tumin, when from a normative point of view, he judges this situation unfavorable to social harmony. I think also, as he does, that it is really possible through appropriate social action, to reduce these inequalities and consequently, to diminish the role of the alternative "captor-captive" in social relationships.

But this coupling of situations is so inherent to the human condition, as I have tried to show it, that it seems impossible to see its total disappearance. The sources of inequalities between men, even if we are able to realize equality before law, in opportunities, and of income distribution, will remain very numerous. I shall try to give evidence of that later.

In spite of my general adherence to Professor Tumin's conception, let me be allowed to begin the discussion with a dissent concerning warfare. It seems to me that mitigation or restriction in the full utilization of military power, and more generally, rules of warfare, are not anomalous from a realistic and even moral point of view, moral behavior being defined objectively as a seeking for general and long-range efficiency. I would agree with Professor Tumin if war were a "zero-sum-two-person-game" or to express the same thing in more simple terms, a pure duel. But war is not "zero-sum" and a lot of collective and individual protagonists are concerned. The consequence is that laws of war and their observance are, to a certain extent, logical and rational. The same reasoning may apply to the rules of economic behavior.

As to power, Professor Tumin defines it as "the capacity to realize one's own ends." It implies purposeful relations with other individuals (or groups). It seems to me that essentially power is a particular phenomenon of social communication. It does not necessarily imply use of force, or even threaten to use it. It generally consists of the transmission of information which is constraining—in the sociological meaning—for the receiver.

More precisely, we may say that an individual (or group considered as an entity) is endowed with power when he is able, by the information he gives to other individuals (or groups) to influence the behavior of these individuals (or groups) in compliance with his own objectives.

It also appears to be useful for our purpose to distinguish between inorganic power and institutionalized authority. I agree with Professor Tumin when he asserts that in the organization of the society we have to reduce imbalance in power distribution and to increase partnership behavior.

But authority, even in the most egalitarian society, remains necessary and, consequently, it does suggest a certain amount of captivity, especially for the political minority. For, in society, ends are complex and fundamental objectives are heterogeneous, not reducible through a rational conversion table one to another (e.g., security, welfare, culture, liberty and equality itself, etc.). Besides, individual ends are recognized to a certain extent, as social values: the fundamental aim of the whole society is the blooming of the individual (this differs with the biological organisms where there are no proper ends of their components). Since our resources and means are limited, these heterogeneous ends or objectives are competing and it is necessary to make them coherent and compatible at a certain level of possibilities. Then we find that the essential function of social authority is to arbitrate among ends, to fix priorities and levels of attainment. Since this arbitration cannot result only from science, expertise and calculation, only a human decision integrating the maximum of human values and experience can perform it.

Of course, the spring of authority must be "pure," that is to say, it must emanate from the people, more precisely from its majority, not from a king "by the grace of God," neither from a "charismatic" leader.

But, since unanimity in the establishment of the scale of values and conversion tables between ends is impossible and not desirable, there always will be disputes, conflicts and tensions in human societies (compare Professor Tumin's concept of "cumulative relative deprivation" and Professor Raymond Aron's concept of "satisfaction querelleuse").

Tensions are necessary for progress. They have to be canalized, not suppressed. Unanimity in a group is a very suspect situation. Democracy is a means to organize without violence and threats, the expression and use of social tensions, to manage a pacific struggle for power. That is to say that democratic means can be used to define the hierarchy of ends and essential ways of action.

In other words, since the society is not spontaneously self-regulating, it requires organs of regulation or control. A certain amount of centralized power is necessary to determine the fundamental options (which I call pre-regulation). But decentralization of authority (co-regulation, auto-regulation) is necessary, not only for a satisfactory distribution of power (participation in decision-making and responsibility), but also for efficiency (economy in communication systems and information processing). And, finally, a post-regulation (or feed-back), partly centralized, is necessary to correct, adapt or refine the pre-regulation and discipline the auto-regulation.

But due to the difficulty of defining and classifying heterogeneous objectives of the society—and consequently of delegating power—politico-administrative systems have a tendency to hypercentralization and there is a risk of social oppression and technical inefficiency. A bureaucratic organization, in the pejorative meaning of the word, is a system where decentralization of decisions and initiative is weak and also where information comes back or climbs up with difficulty. There is a deficiency of co-regulation and of post-regulation (or feed-back). In order to be able to decentralize, we must make an effort for a better definition and comparison of ends and to establish a better hierarchy between them (axiology or teleology would be an aspect of social invention).

Bureaucracy, however, also presents its advantages, as Michel Crozier has shown in his book *Le Phénomène Bureaucratique*. By instituting general objectives and a "sine ira et studio" exercised authority, by suppressing face-to-face relations, it protects to a certain extent, individual freedom and dignity. A rational bureaucracy, in the good acceptance of the word, is a means for a satisfactory minimization of the antagonism captor-captive. In a way, I am captor and captive in a bureaucratic system, or in my relations with it. But I capture or I am captured by law or impersonal rules. Then the capture is more tolerable and if a bureaucratic organization is not favorable to initiative and significant endeavor, it makes no use of fear or hatred.

III. Sources of Inequality and Captivity Other than Power

The inequality that results from differences in aptitudes and talents can only be reduced, not suppressed. Yet I think that intelligence may be increased by learning and real differences between men are less important than they appear.

Improving the distribution of opportunities for education and training is one of the best weapons against inequality and captivity, especially against technical and cultural captivity.

But emotion, feeling, and especially love are important sources of captivity and consequently of inequality. The root or spring of emotion resides precisely in the situation of captor and captive (compare the words "charm," "charmed" [from the Latin word "carmen," meaning "poem," in the sense of a primitive magic incantation to establish one's domination over somebody], "rapt," "rapture," "ravi," "transporté"; "attract," "attrait," "attractive"; "seduce" and "seducere" [the Latin word meaning to separate somebody from his ties and lead with one's self, etc."]).

This captivity is obvious in friendship, love, and, a fortiori, sexual relations. In sexual libido, we find "libido dominandi" and libido of being dominated. Power and sex are alike, as Professor Tumin says.

But here again, it is possible to perceive the possibility of reducing the antagonism of captor-captive. The time will probably come where there will be a distinction between sexual relations, guided by a new ethics and aesthetics, and controlled procreation. Then there will be a certain desacralization of love and sexuality, decreasing of social control, and consequently the reduction of captivity in that sphere of human relations.

I think this "desacralization" is also probable—and desirable—as far as it concerns the family. The family, with the traditional image of the father, as a sacred institution, is an important source of inequality and captivity, especially for wives and children. It is also obvious that the present economic function of the family combined with the mechanism of inheritance is a spring of cumulative unequal distribution of wealth and opportunities. Of course, you may propose to suppress inheritance, abolish private property and even choice in expenditure. But deprived of its economic base, and sooner or later, of the greater part of its educational function, what then does remain of the family: a game of emotional and "captivant" relations?

Finally, however, and with the risk of appearing unduly conservative, after these subversive statements or questions, I believe in a certain permanence of family structures and this seems also to be desirable.

I think that the family is a good milieu in which to build the child and to build the man, because the family tends to integrate a complex set of heterogeneous aims, activities and feelings. It requires foresight, organization, continuity, and reliability. Also, it implies a lot of constraints, but constraints are necessary for successful action and even for freedom.

If the family is to subsist in a free society, there remain certain unequal relationships within it. But now one wonders whether certain organized and controlled forms of inequality are not desirable even for those who undergo this inequality, I think, especially, in the areas of education and learning. Of course the relations of parents to children, or teachers to pupils, can be uselessly authoritarian or hypocritically permissive, as Professor Tumin clearly explained.

But in the situations where free experimentation on the part of the child, pupil or trainee may cause irreparable damage, especially to himself, authority is legitimate. It may be expedient to let a young dog eat shoe polish (in order that the animal builds for itself its list of good and bad things to eat), but not rat poison. Finally, if power and even institutionalized and juridically defined authority may be contested in a certain way, I agree with the statement of Simone de Beauvoir in her book *Pour une Morale de l'ambiguité*, to the effect that the only form of power which cannot be criticized, in principle, is the authority exercised by parents over children and by teachers over pupils. Of course authority has drawbacks. But the development of man is principally during childhood and the absence of learning and discipline would cause irreversible damage.

More generally apprenticeship of life must be performed in a reassuring or sheltering milieu. The child becomes progressively aware of the awful, sad, absurd and helpless side of the human condition on the knees of his grandmother who tells to him horrible stories of giants or wolves that eat children. Here the dipole captor-captive takes the aspect of protector-protected and initiator-initiated.

Finally, it seems to me that it is impossible to reconcile absolutely radical equality and full opportunity of development for the individual. A "residue" of inequality is necessary to preserve essential aspects of liberty. And conversely and more obviously, a lot of constraints, especially of the institutional and judicial type, are required to promote significant and concrete equality.

IV. Conclusion

Finally, I think that in an open, dynamic, evolving society, social change is due to the effects of tensions which can be expressed by the dipoles of cooperation-conflict, consensus-opposition, integration-dissidence, and, finally, captor-captive.

Tensions are necessary for progressive evolution. Man is an ever-contesting animal. But turnover must be expressed through organized channels of communication, if possible—without denying the right to insurrection for the oppressed through physical force and violence, if necessary.

It seems to me that this interesting theoretical concept of captor-captive may be usefully applied to the solution of some aspects or elements of the "social problem." But, in my opinion, the practical solution does not reside in an attempt to eliminate captivity completely. I think it is not possible and perhaps not desirable.

The ways and means in that field are not only reduction of this antagonism, but also reciprocity and turnover for the irreducible part of it. If I am simultaneously or successively captor and captive in different situations and if these positions are approximately equally distributed, both in time and level, the "social game" may be considered as equitable.

Besides, this reciprocal distribution of captivity is also an element of an acceptable solution to the problem of organized authority.

Society may be considered as a cybernetic system. It is fundamentally composed of a set of regulating organs and a set of regulated effectors. To the question, "Who regulates the regulators?" we must be able to answer, one day, if we are to live in a free society: the regulated.

Then the captives will have captured their captors.

COMMENTARY

IRVING ROSOW

Dr. Tumin's brilliant analysis continues his deep and long-standing concern with the costs of all social injustice; in this case, he explores what the unequal power in any social relationship exacts from the system and its members—individuals or groups, organizations or nations. For the price of inequality is imposed on all of us, not only on the disadvantaged. He argues that if *anybody* suffers, then ultimately we *all* do. (Though certainly not in equal measure, for some suffer these penalties in a comfort to which the rest of us can only aspire.) Today, the clamorous pressures for social change are virtually universal among the deprived, and the forces they generate are well nigh irresistible. As Tumin indicates, it is not a matter of whether there will be change, but only what the kind of change will be. To this, as to most of his analysis, I echo a strong "Amen!"

But there are other problems of balance, of generality, of emphasis, and exhaustiveness that warrant another look. From the provocative feast that Tumin spreads before us, I would like to begin with one basic issue: whether *all* social inequality is necessarily bad. In the simplest terms, is unequal social power intrinsically unjust and invariably harmful?

Tumin argues essentially that they are. He indicates that unequal power inevitably subverts the attainment of institutionalized social goals. It is always disfunctional, he implies, if only because it creates conflicting interests, unequal investments in a system, and thereby deviance and strain. One should add that superior power may also corrupt to the extent that it encourages the untrammeled pursuit of self-interest at others' expense.

But the main question is not whether unequal power may aid the cause of injustice, for this is clear, but whether injustice is its *primary* effect. Tumin's analysis indicates that injustice is the main end which inequality serves. While he does not make it explicit, this is the thrust of his argument. First, it is implicit in his very metaphor of captor-captive. Second, the strains that attend unequal power certainly involve problems of distributive justice. Finally, the analysis encompasses an extreme range of relationships from the most intimate within the family to the most impersonal ones of the largest social aggregates. In other words, in order to generalize the specific connection between power imbalance and injustice under all conditions, he offers a single definitive analysis for asymmetrical power relationships *per se*. Despite *a pro forma* disclaimer that other factors are also significant, his analysis proceeds as if sheer power were the main determinate of role relations across a broad range of institutions—whether we are dealing with individuals, families, classes, races or nations; whether with parents and children, social workers and clients, wealthy and poor, Whites and Negroes; or whether the world's advanced and underdeveloped countries. As far as power relationships are concerned, presumably all cases are analytically comparable, governed by the same forces, and subject to the same propositions. His basic position is certainly tenable, and Tumin makes an effective, persuasive—indeed, almost a compelling —case for it.

But there are genuine problems of emphasis, and his analysis definitely seems overdrawn and exaggerated. He might protest that the burden of his interest is qualitative rather than quantitative, that he is concerned only with the correlates of power imbalance, not its potency relative to other factors in shaping social relationships. But this is quite ambiguous and becomes a matter of interpretation rather than definition. Three discussants independently found an inordinate—even depressing—weighting of the power element in human affairs. Tumin's analysis certainly suggests that unequal power always has poor consequences. And if this is his implicit premise, then we can confront it directly and ask if this is invariably so. Does unequal power necessarily and inevitably have bad effects?

Here, incidentally, we will not traffic in the idiom of the white supremacists or any other elite apologists which Tumin has so properly scored. We will not defend unequal social power on any grounds, whether of tradition, the white man's burden, natural endowment, bureaucratic efficiency, benevolent paternalism, patent law, divine grace or whatever. Indeed, we are not defending unequal power on moral grounds at all.

But the simplest functional considerations indicates that social equality and inequality both have advantages and disadvantages, strengths and weaknesses, costs and returns system. It is not simply a matter of equality being good and inequality bad. There are functional and disfunctional aspects of equality, and functional and disfunctional effects of inequality; a complete picture must take all of them into account.

Tumin has examined only the *negative* aspects of *unequal* power. He has not considered any of its positive functions, not even those connected with the sheer division of labor. For example, those who supervise large numbers of people actually require more power in order to do a job than those supervising few. Some inequality of power and authority is simply based on the unequal responsibilities of different positions in the division of social and economic labor. Unequal power is necessary in the coordination of complex social processes and the integration of large enterprises, whether these involve the operation of a ship, a university, a corporation or a metropolis. Superior power in these contexts not only denotes greater authority and responsibility, but may also certify superior competence and expertise. Thus, power, including *bargaining* power for services, may discriminate relative quality. Greater power also serves to control and limit possibly destructive conflict between subordinate competitors. Furthermore, those with more power often exemplify standards and provide role models for those with less. Indeed, in terms of Tumin's students and teachers, it is not the sheer arbitrary power of teachers that students resent so much as the exercise of power by teachers whom they cannot respect. When students can identify with a superior teacher, the power difference is not problematic to anyone and their loyalty and allegiance can become almost frighteningly intense.

This is not a systematic analysis, but almost a haphazard selection that illustrates some of the positive functions of inequality. Professor Pusić has suggested others. In a similar vein, one could indicate some disfunctional aspects of social equality and predict how equal power could also subvert institutionalized social goals. While Tumin's analysis of many negative effects of unequal power is certainly correct, this is not the whole story. For our purposes, the main point is that *social inequality is not invariably invidious, egocentric, self-serving, destructive and unjust.* Inequality is often, but, not always, bad.

If this is so, the problem then becomes, what are the conditions under which unequal power is undesirable. When does superior power become most problematic and serve the cause of injustice? In other words, when *is* inequality bad? The relevant conditions are quite encompassing, but surely include various sources, uses, handling and effects of unequal power. We can indicate only several of the more salient here which reflect basic social values about the nature of justice and proper goals in a democratic society. These conditions also specify some of my criteria of the good and bad in a free social order.

The first factor concerns *how* power is exercised. Unequal power is perhaps most indefensible when it simply follows the dictum that might makes right. The *process* of decision making then is based solely on inequality; no mechanisms to regulate inequities, to appeal decisions or to review action are built into the system to redress injustice.

A second factor concerns the *quality* of the exercise of power. Superior power serves the cause of injustice when it violates human dignity, attacking the basis of someone's self-respect and his sense of worth as a human being. This includes any action that—because of power differences—degrades or humiliates another, that offends his self-esteem, and that functions to demean, to diminish and to destroy another's integrity.

Inequality is also corrupt to the extent that it is purely *self-serving* and becomes an end in itself. This mode inevitably involves the indiscriminate dominance and exploitation of others, and enforces their exclusion from values to which they have a legitimate moral claim.

Related to self-serving inequality is the maintenance of unequal power through the *purposive restriction* of the life-chances of others to appropriate opportunities and rewards, and to full social participation. In other words, superior power is corrupt when it engenders *second-class citizenship* in any form. This does not imply that all social rewards must necessarily be equal, but simply that everyone should enjoy an equal chance to earn them.

Unequal power is unjust if it rests on a person's *ascribed characteristics*—those natural attributes with which he is born—and which are used as the basis of invidious distinctions between groups. At the moment, the most vicious of these are race, caste, and ethnocentrism. There has always been a problem about inequalities because of a person's age or sex. To the extent that ascribed characteristics are linked with visible physical features, the temptation to stigmatize is always present whenever there is any competition for scarcities. Ascriptive power is the first instrument for the manipulation of privilege. It arbitrarily orders the nominal value of men which their other qualities are powerless to dispel.

Finally, unequal power may be unjust if it is based primarily upon dominating economic productivity. In simple economies, the control of economic scarcities often affects the ability to survive, and such control confers the power over the means of survival. The competition for economic scarcities sharpens all other antagonisms and conflicts, placing an additional premium on superior power. But in an advanced economy, the volume of goods and services is not similarly constrained by technical or other objective limitations. Science and technology tremendously increase the alternatives open and enhances the prospect of reordering social priorities. In an advanced economy, there is a characteristic increase in the premium placed on the production of *non-economic values*. Our own economic development has reached the point where the creation of artistic and physical beauty, the discovery of scientific truth, and the rendering of public service *can* have greater social utility than marginal increments of economic value—and be awarded accordingly. At least the possibilities exist to develop more intensively the non-material spheres of life.

A free democratic society is ostensibly concerned with many of these non-economic goals. Accordingly, to the extent that they become feasible, the creation of non-economic values should be increasingly rewarded with significant amounts of power independent of that based on the production of economic market values. Superior power will be unjust if it does not reflect the new options steadily opening before us.

In response to injustices such as the foregoing, it is possible, of course, to press for a circulation of elites so that new groups might then enjoy the fruits of domination. Clearly, such a re-distribution of power could serve the significant function of social restitution. This is certainly relevant if one insists that once a society acknowledges that it has been grievously unjust to some of its members, then it is morally responsible to compensate those who have been injured, in this case through the re-distribution of power. But at what point are such social debts actually liquidated and old injuries made good—especially when, through a circulation of elites, the prime beneficiaries are not the actual victims themselves, but mainly their descendants? This problem contains some of the inherent dilemmas of the Code of Hammurabi.

Even more importantly, mere circulation of elites may not change the principles by which a system or society operates. New groups may succeed to power, but the social order may remain essentially the same. Ironically, perhaps, most power struggles in the world today are less concerned with the principles that govern social relations (i.e., genuine value conflicts) than with the distribution of available values—the division of the pie. In other words, conflict tends to center more on *who* gets the bigger share than on *what* is gotten. Indeed, to old revolutionaries who still try to nurse illusions about their tarnishing ideals, it is distressing how often the *nouveaux puissants*, the ex-underdogs, operate precisely with the values and techniques of the elites they replaced. Today men are not splitting many heads over the principles that govern man's relation to man, for there is considerable unfortunate consensus about them, and generally the intrinsic nature of any social order is called into question much less than one's own particular place in it. Therefore, with a simple circulation of elites, new inequalities may follow the same principles as the old and continue to preserve the former injustices, and only different groups may fill the same old roles in a society. The cast of characters changes, but the play remains the same. It is not enough simply to shrug this off on the basis of social Darwinism or "historical imperatives" or the ruthless impersonality of competitive self-interest. Such a re-distribution of power not only obscures some other possible goals of social change, but also completely ignores the historical context of the present problems of injustice.

Even at this juncture, certain things are quite apparent. From the strictly practical standpoint of social action, it is not crucial whether injustice is an *inevitable* or only a highly *probable* result of inequality. Certainly the two are strongly connected and conflict intensifies their relationship. This link poses a tactical or political problem of social change. The general issue is whether it makes sense for *us* to replace one arbitrary kind of inequality and injustice with another. What will we gain? Are there other alternatives open to us? Tumin's answer points in one direction and mine in another. Although our differences start as *tactical*, they may well be more *consequential* than that implies.

In effect, because inequality is the major force in injustice, Tumin proposes to strike at all unequal power regardless of the cost. In the re-distribution of power, new groups will rise, and their succession will definitely entail many risks:

The *nouveaux puissants* will be inept, untutored, unskillful and clumsy, and will only make matters worse for everyone ... The new rich will be vulgar, banal, sentimental and tawdry in their choices ... One may confidently expect outlandish inefficiencies, misuses of funds, new kinds of nepotisms, temporary if not enduring losses in many desired values and outcomes.

Tumin is inclined to dismiss such results as relatively minor and irrelevant, but I regard them as genuinely significant. The major problem arises precisely from the value conflicts that they engender —what social ends do such costs actually buy.

Tumin has reduced the apparent choices to a patrician-plebeian metaphor, almost to a caricature of the haves and have-nots, of the washed and the unwashed, of the aristocracy and the mob. He speaks of the costs of a fundamental re-distribution of power in terms of the loss of skills and pleasures peculiar to decadent aristocrats, of the destruction of "all the fine things which the old rich had presumably created and, which, unfortunately, could only be properly enjoyed by them." He then observes that, "One may admire and respect the refinement and delicacy in tastes and sensibilities of the privileged elite. But one has to wonder how much they are worth if the total value context in which they have traditionally flourished has involved the degradation, exploitation and barbarization of the lives of the many."

Historically, these have indeed been unfortunate terms of the choice—stark and elemental class conflict, recalling in the modern surge for national independence among underdeveloped colonies the dark days of the French Revolution. Then, inequality rested on basic economic scarcity. If not a literally slave state, French society was a highly polarized class system in which tiny propertied minorities exploited huge disfranchised majorities.

But are these mutually exclusive terms of choice necessary today? Are these our options now? Is this the context of power and other differentials in contemporary America? Are we dominated by crushing *scarcities* that severely limit our choices and result in the exploitation of large majorities by small minorities?

On the contrary. Although the seriously deprived Americans are an important sizable group, we must recognize that they are, nonetheless, a minority in a large society of affluence. And affluence confers upon us significant freedom in the selection of social values. We can address ourselves to broad goals of social change that our knowledge, technology and productivity now make feasible. We may even decide that it is possible to dispense with rapacity as a guiding principle of social order. If we wish, we can choose to divert one-fourth or less of our annual military expenditures to the increase of personal incomes so that no American has to live in destitution and degradation. Or if we feel that we absolutely must, we can even decide to have both guns and butter. And we have other choices as well. In a word, race riots in the Hough ghetto are not the necessary correlates or costs of the Cleveland Orchestra.

Affluence simply is not scarcity. This is the most essential touchstone for the evaluation of Tumin's metaphor of differential power. Affluence makes the polarization of aristocracy and mob, or patrician and plebeian, an over-simplification. When no compelling scarcities are involved, we are free to choose our goals and the principles of their internal distribution. To insist that we eliminate all unequal power despite the costs and regardless of the "new kinds of nepotisms [and] temporary if not enduring losses in many desired values and outcomes" is to ignore the nature and conditions of the choices open to us. Do we really have to prefer one beneficiary of injustice to another or one victim to another? Is this necessary? Is it possible to define goals and develop policies that reduce injustice as such —not only for present or former victims of power, but for all members of the society? Is it possible to concentrate on the substance of injustice in any form, including that which develops from inequalities of power? Is it possible to make the eradication of injustice a major goal of planned change? If we concentrate on the elimination of injustice as such, regardless of cause, we can avoid a lot of confusion about means and ends, about the relationship between inequality and injustice, about whether they are perfectly or only partially synonymous. We can address any given social problem directly without any unnecessary assumptions to haggle about.

This is the crux of my difference with Tumin's emphasis. He is willing to concentrate almost exclusively on the elimination of all *inequality.* But this seems too arbitrary and confining. I believe that it risks unnecessary serious costs that deflect us from other grave social problems. I would prefer to focus on *injustice* as such, including that which is due to inequality, as a means of keeping our social objectives clear and under constant review. But the complexities of this problem require a separate analysis to which the present discussion is merely a prelude.

THE RESPONSE

MELVIN TUMIN

Ladies and gentlemen, we have just heard fine samples of the three distinctive intellectual traditions which are characteristic of the three different countries from which the gentlemen come.

Dr. Pusić, for instance, showed the kind of penetration into the question of the objective versus the subjective determinants of behavior which stems from the constant awareness which those raised in the Marxist tradition have learned and contributed so importantly to all our thinking; unfortunately, not enough of our thinking shows concern for the objective base.

Dr. Mehl's contribution illuminates the kind of beauty and grace that comes from starting with the supposition of a non-value-containing but self-evaluating existential world in which the consequences of action determine the values of the action. Starting with this kind of existential position we are led to a series of conclusions in Dr. Mehl's paper that serve as extremely important modifications and criticisms of what I said. Please note that in true Gallic fashion, Dr. Mehl is totally consistent except when it comes to the analysis of family life. There, according to him, we find inherent values. I find in this idea a very nice inconsistency.

Dr. Rosow's paper, unfortunately cut short by lack of time, was a beautiful illustration of the strength and the wisdom of a modest version of functional sociology or functionalist analysis. Applied to social behavior, this analysis asks not only what "good" does any action bring, but what "bad" does it bring as well. Such an approach always gives us a view of the balance of events that enables us to at least clarify our choices and make our judgments better. If we can see both the prices and profits of our actions, which functionalist analysis helps us to do, we are then able to make wiser choices and wiser decisions, even though we may not agree with each other about what values ought to be taken into account.

The three visions, then, I find extremely illuminating and I wish I'd had all of them in my paper. I am delighted with Dr. Pusić's broad vision that asks us to extrapolate our analysis of inequality in power to higher levels of abstraction and to larger social aggregates. I confined myself to examples of child-adult and Negro-White conflicts in our society. Pusić reminds us of the larger social aggregates and the impersonal forces of the histories that are at work here, and that require us to account for the persistence of power relationships. If we're not going to use an instinctive theory of the origins of the desire for power, and if we take power as given in any social relationship, how do we account for the persistence of particular power arrangements? Here Pusić asks us to look at the particular interests of the powerful who are being served and the inducements of the powerless to obey. The word "inducements" has a little too much voluntaristic tinge for my likes, but that's a matter of language, I'm sure. In any event, Pusić reminds us with considerable seriousness and wisdom that we are witnessing a diminution in the validity of the heretofore objective justification for hierarchy (e.g., highly unequal governmental powers) and for the role of scarcity in determination of social relationships. In effect, this diminished validity of inequality is a basic source of social change. Pusić warns us quite properly of the likelihood that there will be attempts on the part of the powerful to hold onto their power even when the objective grounds vanish. I took as my starting point the situation where the objective grounds no longer seem to be reasonable, when all the negative circumstances pile up so that it is painful to continue in the present relationships. I argued that at such a time we had better reconsider the distributions of power.

Dr. Mehl also went on to generalize in a different way the applicability of the metaphor of the captor and captive to areas where the metaphor is not normally applied. I find it refreshing and illuminating in this regard to think about my power to forgive the world or not to forgive it—which is the ultimate "coolness," it seems to me, the ultimate detachment to stand up in the world and to forgive it because it is not in itself a valuing but only an operating and a conducting organism. This is, of course, the ultimate freedom, one which can be enjoyed by those who sleep under the bridges of the Seine as well as those who sleep in chateaus. Thank goodness, however, for *some* ultimate source of equality, even if it's only on the metaphysical level.

Dr. Mehl, of course, is not fooled into believing that this is the only important freedom. He recognizes the importance of equalities and inequalities in concrete aspects of life and he argues for the probable necessity of inequalities in power where authority is necessary for efficiency. Here I have to raise the question, "What does efficiency mean?" Does efficiency have a scope that includes a wide number of values and not simply the productive goals of one particular manager? In any event, efficiency is not, *per se*, better than inefficiency. It all depends what other values are at stake. I think we ought never to take for granted efficiency as a value *per se*. We often treat it as a value that governs all other values. Yet we must always ask, "Efficient for what?"

Mehl points to the requirement of unequal power in situations where values that are desired by all can be achieved only if there is inequality and I don't doubt that this condition applies in love relationships and other relationships as they are now given. I suggest, however, that many of them produce a price as against the profit which is so overbearing for so many of the participants that other forms of relationships might better be sought, forms that might yield a higher positive value quotient to everyone concerned.

For instance, while there are surely certain kinds of extraordinary pleasures which derive both for man and woman in the love and sex relationship as now organized by most of our norms, I do not think there is anything so given in nature that requires that this is the only form in which its pleasures can be forthcoming. One can think of the experiments with which the more liberated younger generations confront us, in which, for instance, we are now being asked to consider the likelihood of the traumatizing of parents by the inverse oedipus complex; where, instead of children being witnesses to the primal scene of their parents, the parents are now being witnesses to the primal scene among their children. Who knows what pleasures might lie ahead if we were to consider these? Less facetiously, I suggest the likelihood of new positive pleasures for all of us that might ensue from more open exploration. There is a new possible freedom in learning, for instance, not to care what your children do.

There are, of course, new prices to be paid in new relationships. Dr. Mehl argues that the socialization of the young, especially the prevention of irreversible damages for the young, requires unequal power for parents. We could surely agree with this, if we could predict what would be "irreversible damages." I think of the extraordinary list of possible irreversible damages that each of us starts with in raising our children, who then become tight, dour, pessimistic people who are sure the world is full of dangers because we said, repeatedly, "be careful, be careful, be careful." Our concept of a probable irreversible damage may be a child's notion of a heck of a lot of fun with only little risk. We are urged by these considerations at least to reconsider those notions which have been heretofore defined as fraught with so much danger that children are not allowed to try them.

Dr. Rosow develops further the themes that Dr. Mehl has argued, with regard to the places at which unequal power may be necessary, not only necessary but also just, and not only just but also positive in its consequences for everyone concerned. He asserts the positive functions of unequal power in the running of bureaucracies, in the socialization of children, in the reduction of conflict among persons who might otherwise be engaging in unnecessary and undesirable conflict for everyone concerned. He states that I urged that we strike at unequal powers, regardless. I think this is not so, even though I see how he could have read this implication in my paper, because I deliberately chose to engage in some hyperbole by omission in order to pull our attention away from the apparent desirability of existing relationships.

I want to argue simply and finally that at least in the relationships that I specified, the discontent of the captives (if you don't like the word "captive," call them anything else that you want to— of children, of Negroes, of women, of the poor nations) with existing relationships (with their chances in life as such) is great. Whatever other advantages and virtues, therefore, we may see in the present relationships, whatever hazards we may foresee for ourselves and them in possible changes, we are invited both by their discontent and by the unworkability of the existing relationships, by the low order of yield of pleasurable gain of the existing relationships, to consider gracious withdrawal from our privileged positions, and to plan the redistribution of the powers to participate more effectively and more joyously in the enterprises of which they are members.

Partnership is a very-different relationship from captor-captive or from parent-child. Some of the relationships that we now insist are necessary may not be able to be treated as partnerships. They may have to be conducted as captor-captive. In such cases, we would ask, "Are those relationships necessary?" If the family *per se* involved necessarily some degree of captor-captivity or unequal distribution of power, then at least we ought to raise the question whether the existing form of socialization in rearing of the young is the only possible form under which all the advantages we now accrue could be gained. Or, are there other ways of raising children that might produce children with a different balance of characteristics, that would, from another vision, be just as desirable, if not more so?

Those of us who are dominant in power situations often can't see how the powerless feel. We often cannot sympathize with degradation. We do not know what it means, what it really feels like to be in a position of constant defeat, to shut our mouths when someone says, "Shut up!" We do not know what it means to be on the side of the powerless in terms of not being able to finally fight back except with sullenness, hostility, internal seething and discontent. We confirm our own hypotheses; we tend to verify our own initial premises by selective perception. But there is too much to gain in new explorations in equality to allow ourselves the luxury of such self-deception. I do believe it is time to start these explorations.

IV

THE ESSAY

The Social Sciences and Their Impact on Society

GUNNAR MYRDAL

Professor of International Economics, Institute for International Economic Studies, Stockholm University

COMMENTARY

JULIA J. HENDERSON

Director, Bureau of Social Affairs, United Nations

EVELINE M. BURNS

Professor of Social Work, Columbia University School of Social Work

GEORGE F. ROHRLICH

Visiting Professor of Social Policy, School of Social Service Administration, University of Chicago

THE RESPONSE

GUNNAR MYRDAL

The Social Sciences and Their Impact on Society

GUNNAR MYRDAL

I.

It is a formidably broad subject I have been asked to reflect upon and one about which there is very little scientific knowledge. The sociology of science and technology in general, and that of social science and social engineering in particular, is an underdeveloped discipline. In the almost total absence of research in this field, all we can do is to speculate, trying to put in some systematic order the impressions we have from our work and its practical impact on society. While this obviously entails the risk of going totally wrong or, at best, of only reaching conclusions that are less specific and determinate than the standards we ordinarily try to attain in our work, such speculation is nevertheless the beginning of the search for knowledge: it raises questions and formulates hypotheses for research.

Quite aside from this rationale, we who are professionally engaged in social sciences and technology—and who are not naïve about the meaning of what we are doing, which is not unusual in our profession—can hardly avoid speculating on the topic stated in the title of my lecture. Speaking for myself, this complex of problems has been a major preoccupation of my mind since my early youth, when curiosity about society and the urge to improve it first led me to the study of social facts and relationships. It has remained so for almost a lifetime of work in the field, uninterrupted even by brief excursions into the political arena, where the translation of ideas and knowledge into action for the welfare of society is supposed to take place.

It is appropriate that we social scientists and social engineers ask ourselves this question: what difference does it make to policies and developments in our countries and in the world, if we can increase knowledge about society and liberate men's ideas from ignorance and irrational inhibitions? Perhaps I should make clear before I begin that I will be speaking mainly as an economist, though trying to keep in mind the situation of my colleagues in the other social disciplines.

II.

A second preoccupation, which we share with all fairly educated people in the world, but which to us, as social scientists and engineers, must be especially disturbing, is a general understanding that in our field of study progress is very much slower than in the natural sciences. It is their discoveries and inventions which are compelling radical changes in society, while ours, up till now, have been very much less consequential. There is spreading a creeping anxiety about the dangerous hiatus inherent in this contrast. While man's power over nature is increasing rapidly, and indeed accelerating, man's control over society—which means in the first place over his own attitudes and institutions—is lagging far behind. In part, at least, this is due to a slower pace in the advance of our knowledge about man and his society, the fundamental knowledge that can then be translated into action for social reform.

Let me, therefore, start out by raising the more fundamental question of why advance in the social sciences is so much slower than in the natural sciences. One possible explanation would be that the students of natural phenomena are brighter than we who labor in the social sciences. In the total absence of research on the selective processes by which young people are channelled into one or the other field of research, we cannot exclude this possibility. Nothing succeeds like success, we know, and the very rapid advance in natural sciences (to which I also reckon medicine) definitely lends them prestige and glamour. Moreover, those who enter upon a career as students in the natural sciences have the prospect of greater immaterial and material rewards—provided they have superior intelligence and are lucky.

The tremendous acceleration of advance in the natural sciences during the last two generations could be expected to give rise to a vicious circle in which ever smaller proportions of a nation's superlatively gifted young people entered the social sciences and ever larger proportions entered the natural sciences. As the inflow of genius in the natural sciences would rise, our intake of comparable quality would decline, and this would continually decrease further our chances of keeping pace with them.

I should not be honest with my audience if I did not confess that I have the impression that this is what has happened during my lifetime and is still happening. Our profession is swelling even if not so fast as that of natural scientists and technologists, but it seems to recruit a rising share of mediocre students and, more importantly, attracts fewer of that small minority in every generation who are endowed with the rare combination of mental and physical stamina, will power, adventurousness and high intelligence, that engenders radical departures from conventional approaches and produces great discoveries and inventions.

When I say this, I should add that it is merely a scientifically uncontrolled induction from the unassorted experiences gathered while living and working as a social scientist with many friends among the natural scientists. I might be wrong. Let me state that we don't need to be in doubt about the facts. I consider it one of the many indications of the general dullness and relative absence of fresh departures in the pursuit of social sciences at present, that this important problem of the recruitment to the various sciences has not been investigated and, worse still, that the problem has usually not been recognized to exist by social scientists.

I should also add that what I judge to be the present intellectual depression in the social sciences might prove to be only a passing conjuncture. The threatening trends of change in human affairs— I am thinking, for instance, of the nuclear and the less publicized chemical and biological armament race, of the pending hunger crisis in the underdeveloped countries, and, in a country like the United States, the rapid physical and moral deterioration of the cities and the rising temperature in interracial relations—might again attract more students of the adventurous, independent-minded, and highly intelligent type, whom we need in order to make radically new departures and generally to raise standards in our research.

III.

But our less fortunate recruitment opportunities—if my hunch is correct—cannot be the only reason why the social sciences are lagging. The problems we deal with are truly more difficult to solve than those in the natural sciences. For one thing, the method of experimentation is denied us. This is, of course, true even in astronomy. The more fundamental difficulty is that we don't have the constants which, for instance, permit a physicist like Albert Einstein and, indeed, the whole profession of physicists, to make fundamental discoveries at their writing desks by simply applying mathematical reasoning to a limited number of ascertained facts.

If we economists, for instance, establish by observation the income or price demand elasticity for sugar, it is valid only for one social group of consumers in a single community at a particular date—not to mention the fact that the concept itself loses what I call adequacy to reality and thereby analytical usefulness in underdeveloped countries that have no markets or only very imperfect ones.

In recent times, there has been a strenuous and strained effort by many of my colleagues to emulate the methods of the natural sciences, though in constructing their simplified models they usually require only the elementary type of mathematics taught in high schools, or at least in European high schools. This is now the fashion in economics and increasingly also in the other social sciences which, in their turn, seek to emulate economics.

Fashion changes in a cyclical way in our field of study. My first visit to the United States as a young man coincided with the appearance of what was then called the "new economics," or the institutional school. I foresee that, ten or fifteen years from now, the institutional approach will again be the new vogue, and that the recent attempts to emulate the methods of the simpler natural sciences will be recognized as a temporary aberration into superficiality and irrelevance.

My reason for making this forecast is that the study of social facts and relationships really must concern much more complex and fluid matters than facts and relationships in nature; that, in social study, we do not have constants similar to those of the natural sciences is an indication of the deeper truth that, in our field, human institutions and attitudes are prominent in the causal relationships. These phenomena can be represented only very partially by parameters and variables in simplified models of causal relationships; indeed, they are much more difficult even to observe and measure as facts.

This is true even in the highly developed countries where there are fairly perfect markets (in the sense the economists give this term), implying that attitudes and institutions have been rationalized to the extent of permitting us to assume that they give fairly free passage for social change or that they rapidly adjust to such change. But even in a country like Sweden, where this process of rationalization has gone further than even in the United States, it has been demonstrated, for instance, that mobility in the labor market—and, still more, changes in the prices of labor—are less exclusively and simply dominated by demand and supply than model thinking has to assume.

Abstraction from attitudes and institutions, as well as modes and levels of living, in the economic analysis of underdeveloped countries carried out in the ordinary method, utilizing simple aggregative terms of incomes, savings, employment, investment and output, leads to grossly inadequate and seriously biased inferences. After working for nine years on a study of the development problems in South Asia, I feel to my dismay that it is very much open to doubt whether the aid to planning given by the economic profession has helped more than it has hurt these unfortunate, poor and backward new nations. The contribution of the other social sciences has been up till now mostly irrelevant and of little practical importance for planning policies.

More generally, in emulating the methods of natural sciences, we exclude from consideration everything related to the fact that human beings have souls. Specifically, we tend not to appreciate the fact that people live in a complex system of institutions which manifest sharply differentiated combinations of changeability and rigidity, according to the attitudes that have been moulded by, at the same time as they support or react against, these institutions. This failure has led to a particularly dangerous type of superficiality in approach, namely, an unawareness of the assumptions upon which the analysis is based. When scrutinized by logical criticism, the reasoning of the model builders, which is proudly paraded as if it were in some particular degree "strict" and "rigorous," is regularly found to be lacking in logical consistency as well as in adequate relevance to reality.

In other words, it is simply loose and muddled thinking disguised in a straightjacket of pretended exactitude. It represents an approach which is greatly assisted psychologically by a naïveté in regard to both the sociology and the philosophy of knowledge that has always characterized the social scientists. Historically, this naïveté is related to the fact that our sciences once emerged as branches of the metaphysical moral philosophies of natural law and utilitarianism and the simplicist hedonistic psychology. In order to free itself from these damaging legacies, the new institutional approach in the social sciences, the emergence of which I look forward to, will have to make a major effort to clarify the concepts and improve the logic which we employ. In a true sense, it will have to be more strict and more rigorous.

When I drafted this lecture, I was just finishing the last part of my book on South Asia, which deals with the qualitative aspects of the population problem, health and education. The chapter on health can be quite straightforward and simple in its approach; health is a biological phenomenon and there exists a medical science and a medical technology that is valid for all people and even for animals. But no such exact science and technology of education exists and cannot, for reasons I have alluded to, ever be expected to exist. When in recent years economists belatedly became interested in education as a factor in economic development—and, in the typical fashion of present-day social science, constructed simplified models in terms of "investment in man"—the exercise turned out to be not even a formulation of the real problems in education to be solved by social scientists, if we want to take due consideration of education as an important development factor.

IV.

Another cause of greater difficulties in social research is related to the role of value premises for that research. In principle, it is true that all scientific and technological work has to be based on value premises. But in the field of natural phenomena, the value premises are both simple and evident—*a priori*. Basic research can branch off in every direction where knowledge can be advanced; applied research has the simple criterion of profitability or, as in medical technology, the prevention of death, and, prior to that, the prevention and cure of disease. This is not so in the social field where valuations are immensely diversified and anything but self-evident. In order to avoid biases in research and to make it "objective" in the true sense, we need explicit and concrete value premises, not only to draw meaningful and correct practical, that is to say technological inferences, but also in order to ascertain relevant facts and factual relationships.

I am here touching on the main methodological problem of the social sciences. Without being able in this brief lecture to give reasons, I have to restrict myself to the assertion that there can never be, and has never been, "disinterested" research in the social field as there can be in physics or other natural sciences. Valuations enter into our work from start to finish even if we manage to be unaware of it; and this is true however much it is directed upon simply observing and recording the facts. A study of Negro voting in the southern parts of the United States is, in the civilizational milieu of that country, confined within the value-loaded concept of discrimination. The fault is not that our approach in research is determined by valuations but that we fail to make ourselves and our readers aware of them by stating them as clear and explicit premises of that research. For unless this is done, we are drawing inferences with one set of premises missing. The value premises should not be defined arbitrarily but must be relevant and significant in the society under study.

The metaphysical moral philosophies from which the social sciences stemmed actually asserted that the valuations could themselves be objective; this was, indeed, the metaphysical element in these philosophies. Traditional social sciences have not broken away from this legacy of false thinking, which, of course, also dominates popular thinking everywhere. What social scientists have done is to conceal the valuations so deeply at the base of their theoretical structures—and in the very terminology they use—that they can happily remain unaware of them in their researches, and easily come to believe that their inferences are merely factual. The hidden valuations remain non-concretized, vague and general; consequently, whenever they are then used in such a way as to imply that they have been given a definite meaning, this meaning and the inferences drawn are unfounded and arbitrary. This is what I mean by saying that social scientists are quite commonly working with one set of premises too few.

Among the social scientists, the economists have, in their so-called welfare theory, provided themselves with a vast and elaborate coverture for their escape from the responsibility to state simply and straight-forwardly, their value premises—a "monumentally unsuccessful exercise ... which has preoccupied a whole generation of economists with a dead end, to the almost total neglect of some of the major problems of our age." [1] It grows like a cancerous tumor; hundreds of books and articles are continuously produced every year on welfare economics, though the whole approach was proved to be misdirected and meaningless at least three decades ago. We should note that this recent flourishing of welfare economics is closely related to the growing predilection for hyper-abstract models: among their implicit and not sufficiently scrutinized assumptions—and sometimes even in their explicit super-structures—the objectified welfare concept almost always plays a major role.

An institutional approach which gives due importance to people's attitudes and institutions, cannot so easily escape the valuations that are at the same time objects of research and implied as premises in research.

V.

These main difficulties in social research—that it must concern attitudes and institutions which in a complex way combine changeability and rigidity, that we therefore have no constants as in the natural sciences, and that valuations enter into research from the beginning to the end—and the escapist ways we have tried to bypass these difficulties, are not unrelated to the fact that so very little

[1] Kenneth E. Boulding, "The Economics of Knowledge and the Knowledge of Economics," *American Economic Review*, Vol. LVI, No. 2 (May, 1966), p. 12.

stands out as undisputed truth in our findings. In regard to all problems there are schools of thought with different gospels, among which the politicians and the citizens at large can choose according to their predilections. It has even become a popular stereotype that economists never agree; if the same view is not so commonly expressed about the other social scientists, it is only because people apparently care less about what they are saying.

When more than sixty years ago Knut Wicksell, now recognized as the great economist of his time, gave his lecture on the occasion of his ascendancy to the chair in economics at Lund University, he began by stating that economics, "like theology and for approximately the same reasons," had failed to arrive at generally accepted results. It is true, he pointed out, that the history of all sciences is a history of controversy. But in the natural sciences such warfare of ideas usually leads to a definite outcome. Theories are refuted, hypotheses become obsolete, the frontiers of knowledge are pushed forward.

"The Copernican idea of the universe, the Newtonian system, the theory of blood circulation, and the phlogiston theory in chemistry once found both adherents and opponents. Nowadays these theories are either universally believed or disbelieved—provided, in the latter instance, that they have not simply been forgotten."[2] In economics, on the contrary, *all* doctrines live on persistently. No new theories ever completely supplant the old. He gave examples that are all equally relevant today.

Wicksell, a faithful and almost religious believer in hedonistic psychology and utilitarian moral philosophy, saw the explanation for this unfortunate situation in the fact that we had not succeeded in measuring "utility." If such a thing existed, I believe we should concede that he was right; by measuring it we would advance to the same situation as the natural sciences, have constants, and be able to solve all our difficulties in terms of the maximization of welfare.

But this is exactly what we have not been able to do and never will be able to do, because there is this inescapable logical defect in the very concepts of utility and welfare that "pleasures" and

---

[2] *Ekonomisk Tidskrift*, 1904, pp. 457 ff.

"pains" of people cannot be gauged by a single measuring rod. The only way of defending objectivity in research, of avoiding biases and arbitrariness, and of dissolving the irrational controversies, is to work with explicit, often alternative, specific value premises that are relevant and significant.

Another great economist in the past, Karl Menger, once pointed out that, in a sense and to an extent, the gifted student is superior to his methods. Otherwise, our situation in the social sciences would be much worse than it actually is. Luckily, we see all around us important findings of great practical importance being reached by students whose fundamental notions of methodology are faulty and confused. One of Wicksell's own contributions was, as we know, his early formulation (at the beginning of this century) of the theory we now refer to as Keynes', which explains why we in Sweden, who had been exposed to that theory already in our undergraduate studies, were a little ahead of the rest of the world in regard to the methods of fighting the Great Depression in the 'thirties. That theory is one of the major examples of important ideas and knowledge that to our great advantage is now generally translated into action—recently and, on the whole, with ever more important practical effects even in the United States.

Much more generally our knowledge of social facts and relationships *is* advancing, though not as rapidly as we should wish. The very fact that we are dealing with social data in the rational terms of cause and effect and means and ends implies—in so far as our ways of thinking through education and other media is influencing popular thinking—a gradual liberation of people's preparedness to take action in order to improve society. I will come back to this.

VI.

Not only is knowledge in the social field so much harder to acquire than in the natural sciences but also its translation into action for the welfare of society is a much more cumbersome process. Usually, the invention of a new production technology, often founded upon a discovery reached by basic research in the natural sciences, can rather easily be evaluated in terms of costs and the saleability of new products or services. There are private entrepreneurs eager to make a profit by exploiting the invention; when the state enters the field it evaluates an invention in the same simple and, in a sense, objective way. Rather effortlessly, advances in natural sciences and technologies thus become translated into action for the welfare of society. Both private industries and the state are indirectly involved themselves by initiating and financing research which they expect to be able to exploit to their advantage.

Our discoveries and inventions in the social field must generally be applied first by the collectivities, i.e., the state and subordinate political communities. They must become public policies which are accepted by those who have the power to determine the actions or non-actions of these collectivities. Ordinarily, these people with power have their preconceived ideas. No less ordinarily, these ideas are founded on what they experience as their interests. These ideas might be shortsighted or even erroneous; they do not necessarily, or even commonly, coincide with what would stand out as the public interest of ordinary people if they were all alert and rational; they are what we call "vested interests." And those in power have not the same respect for the social engineers as they do for the technical engineers. They all have their own social theories. The fact that social scientists so often disagree among themselves increases the self-assurance of the policy-makers and provides them with the random opportunity to quote "authority" to support their own preconceptions.

When we want our ideas and knowledge to be translated into action for the welfare of society, we have, therefore, first to convince our colleagues so that we can form a fairly united front, and second, to win enough political support in the lay society for the specific reforms that embody our inventions. These special duties laid upon us social scientists and technologists have little or no correspondence with practice in the field of natural sciences and technologies. In the latter field, unanimity about what is truth follows naturally and rapidly after discovery; there is little need to convert people to utilizing the inventions for their own benefit.

This special position of social scientists and technologists has—in the great tradition—generally been accepted as a challenge. Particularly perhaps in economics, we have spared time from our research work and endeavored to write down our main findings in simple terms that laymen can understand. We have formulated our practical policy conclusions in equally simple terms, and tried to impress them upon those forming policies. The final acceptance—not until the 'sixties—of the Wicksell-Keynes theory as guidance for United States economic policy demonstrated what a long struggle we have to wage in order to have our ideas and knowledge translated into action. But it also shows that that struggle can be won, even if it takes time and effort.

At this point, I have to note with regret how economists and social scientists generally have shown a tendency in recent decades to abandon the tradition—adhered to through generations by even the greatest scholars—that they have a responsibility for the formation of public opinion. They are increasingly addressing only one another. Using knowledge to enlighten the people is not encouraged: young men learn that this might lower their standing and chances for advancement in the profession. They exhibit an unhealthy interest in research technique for its own sake; they avoid taking up politically controversial issues for study, which means that they avoid issues of great practical importance; they focus their studies on terminology, methods of measurement, aimless collection of data and similar other-worldly problems. The model builders are, in particular, prominent in disassociating research from life.

Fundamentally, this is escapism. Even if they convince themselves that it establishes them on a higher level of scientism, the price society pays is that the social scientists become less consequential. When that pattern once becomes established, it lays a wall of inhibition on those who win entrance to our profession, thereby limiting not only their immediate usefulness to society but also, I believe, their research horizon.

Thus, with a few exceptions, neither the professional economists nor the sociologists had much to do with the rather recent—and belated—raising to political importance of the issues of pathological poverty in the United States; and the rapid deterioration of the cities, the threat of intensified racial conflicts, and other developments within the same complex all fell outside their current interests. Partly, the trends were not seen and studied; partly, those few students who saw the writing on the wall and spoke out were not listened to. In both instances, the response did not encourage any student to make these problems a major field of study.

Again, when the superstitious doctrine of budget balancing was broken by political action, and when many equally superstitious ideas related to that fatal metal, gold, gradually lost their grip over Congress and the people, it was publicists, enlightened businessmen and politicians who were more important in causing the break with inherited faith than the many thousands of university economists in this country.

I should make the qualification that even in our time there have been a few professors, like Alvin Hanson and Kenneth Galbraith, who have not only devoted time to enlightening the general public, but also have then not evaded but sought out the issues of needed economic and social reforms. Undoubtedly, their writings, together with a general educational influence from the teaching of the social sciences in colleges and universities, have had importance both for activizing individuals in the other categories mentioned who have been more directly pressing for the reforms and also for preparing the general public for their acceptance. But the reforms mature very much too slowly and are far less perfect than what is needed in our society—a society which is changing with explosive rapidity and often in directions which are creating new and bigger maladjustments.

VII.

My experience in life as a social scientist and a social reformer has thus taken me far away from that simple trust in an easy and rapid advance towards Utopia, which, I confess, I had when I was young and had drunk deeply of the political optimism of Enlightenment. I believe I have not become cynical; I stick to the ideals of that glorious tradition as firmly as ever, but I am less hopeful about their early realization. People's attitudes and institutions are not only important objects for our study, which we can abstract from only at the peril of going seriously wrong scientifically. When trying to translate ideas and knowledge into social reform, what we are up against, in the last instance, is the arduous task of inducing changes in people's attitudes that regularly have a firm institutional anchorage. We are not living in Plato's state, ruled by the philosophers.

I am enough of an Americophile, however, to seek a more hopeful ending of a lecture in which I have given vent to so much honest disillusionment—both about the social sciences and about the possibility of translating our findings into action by social engineering. Let me then first point out that attitudes and institutions are all related to, and depend for their unaltered existence upon, people's beliefs about reality. These beliefs are often grossly irrational. The pursuit of social study and the dissemination of rational findings should tend in time to correct irrational beliefs and thereby unsettle attitudes and institutions.

When white people, even in the South, now must risk appearing uneducated if they adhere to prejudiced and scientifically refuted beliefs about Negroes' physical and mental characteristics, a change has emerged which undoubtedly increases the possibilities of improving race relations. Likewise, the spread of knowledge about pathological poverty of large sections of our society—and about its social and economic costs even to the rest of society—must tend to concern the habitually unconcerned and tend to eventually break down the resistance to social reforms in a very wide field.

Public opinion and even the thinking of social scientists have, as we know, traditionally shown a strong fatalistic tendency in America: a bias towards *laissez-faire*. It had been fortified by several traumatic experiences of policy miscarriage, the two most important of which were first the failure of Reconstruction after the Civil War and then of Prohibition. More fundamentally, this *laissez-faire* bias was a rationalization of what dominant population groups conceived of as their vested interests in the *status quo*.

One reason why, on the whole, it was so seldom effectively challenged was the lack of drive for participation in politics (in the wider sense) by the lower strata of the population, a fact which is illustrated in the generally low percentages of people taking part in elections in the United States or organizing themselves in trade unions. What I call the American "underclass," and have characterized as the world's least revolutionary proletariat, has not played an important role in the United States. It would take me far from the topic of my lecture to try to explain this distinctive trait of

American society. I simply have to restrict myself to asserting, without giving proofs, that when American policies—in regard to taxation, social insurance, and social security generally, including health and child care, minimum wage legislation, agricultural support, housing, and urban renewal—have traditionally been less favorable to the lowest strata than in other, more advanced welfare states, this is not unrelated to the relative passivity of the American "underclass."

What may now be happening is that the political participation of the lower strata in America is increasing at the same time social scientists have been drawn upon to spread knowledge about the costs of the rural and urban slums to the rest of society. It may therefore be possible in time to change the "unconditional war against poverty" from a skirmish consisting of rather unassorted, spurious and, on the whole, minor measures, into a large-scale front with more systematic, planned-policy effort. As this development gathers momentum the majority of Americans in comfortable conditions will be learning in a pragmatic way, aided, I hope, by analyses of social scientists, not only that the slums are a drag on economic growth but also that policy interference against pathological poverty does not ruin America. In some more advanced welfare states, there have been studies supporting the thesis that well-planned social welfare policies are profitable for all social classes.

The tradition in the social sciences in America has been to view attitudes and institutions as merely obstacles to induced change; this is part of the legacy from Veblen. I believe this is wrong, and this should be another reason for hopefulness. The entire attitudinal structure—which I called the American Creed and which is anchored in the Constitution and a whole system of institutions—has always been and will remain, a major force for change; it will continue to function in that capacity and thereby help to destroy other attitudes and institutions of a conflicting character.

These ideals are rationalistic; contrary to the *laissez-faire* tradition they demand reform when social reality does not conform to the ideals. Under their influence, attitudinal and institutional change takes on the character of a moral catharsis; we have seen much evidence of this in recent years regarding the status of the Negro.

As attitudes different from these institutionalized ideals draw part of their support from opportunistic and false beliefs about reality, the intellectual catharsis that follows improved knowledge stimulates and supports the moral catharsis.

When I observe—from some distance—the present trends of policy formation, as well as public opinion, in the United States, I feel that attitudes and institutions are now changing ever more rapidly, on the whole and in spite of occasional setbacks, in the direction of reason and the inherited ideals I referred to—although there is much resistance and double-think. The social scientists and the social engineers play a role in this development and they may be beginning to play it more effectively.

If we are lagging far behind our colleagues in the field of natural sciences and technology, we are equally far ahead of public opinion. With all the faults of our approach to social problems which I have hinted at, we are in one sense rationalistic: we are, as I said, thinking in terms of cause and effect and of means and ends. As soon as we face a social problem, we are—by logical necessity— planners, producing plans for induced changes. We might not have many "inventions," in the narrow sense of that term, to offer, but as spreaders of rationalism and, therefore, of the preparedness for planning induced changes, we play our role. And we will do it more effectively, if we become less timid about tackling practical problems and less prone to escape into scientism.

Sweden—where professors, even of the social sciences, have traditionally enjoyed a higher prestige and have always played a greater role as innovators of policies than their American colleagues—is considerably more advanced as a welfare state than the United States. Sweden has, in the decades during which I have been an observer—and sometimes a participant observer—shown a remarkable and accelerating development towards rationality in regard to the acceptance of planned and induced social change. In Sweden, political parties are becoming part of a "service state," where they compete in urging planning and reforms. The mill of public committees set up to plan induced social change, the activity of the proliferating interest organizations, and the agencies of the political parties—all are grinding out rationally planned reform proposals in ever greater volume but without creating much public stir any longer. This has resulted in a rapid increase of institutional flexibility and in a growing acceptance of the idea that institutions should be judged from the functional point of view, as serving commonly held valuations.

I have no doubt that a similar change is under way in the United States. Though it has not proceeded so far as yet, and though from time to time there are regrettable throwbacks, the United States has moved a long way from Sumner's conviction that "stateways cannot change folkways." Undoubtedly, this development is partly the result of a diffused influence from the social sciences; more importantly, it should open up increasing possibilities for social scientists and technologists to have an impact on the development of society, and even to devote their skills to producing what we more ambitiously might come to regard as "inventions."

VIII.

So far as the internal development of the United States is concerned, I am an optimist and I have always been so. I wish I could be similarly optimistic about its foreign policy. I have in other contexts developed the reasons why foreign policy tends to be even much less guided by rational considerations than internal policy. This is true for all countries; but for a country like the United States—that in a reaction against generations of isolationism has swung to the other extreme of feeling itself responsible for the whole world and so become apt to interfere everywhere—the consequences become much more damaging both for the welfare of its own people and for that of humanity at large.

People's knowledge of conditions in other countries is very much more inadequate than similar knowledge of their own country, and they are unaware of how all sorts of mythological stereotypes have been substituted for knowledge. In the field of foreign relations, there are none of the interest organizations whose competition and cooperation generally tend to promote circumspection that we have within a nation. Emotions are given a freer reign: foreign relations are a field where people can find an outlet for their suppressed hostility and aggressiveness. To stand up for what is presented as the interests and rights of one's own country, or to get tough with any foreign nation which gets in our way, becomes generally acclaimed as displaying national vigor and virtue; it serves as a shortcut to patriotism. As a conflict is hardening, emotionalism can easily reach a stage when reasoning is blinded.

Under the influence of these various factors, decision-making in foreign policy tends—even in a political democracy—to become delegated to a small group of persons at the center. This tendency becomes the stronger the more a conflict—and the consequent emotional heat—escalates by circular causation. The rationalization of this surrender of an independent judgment by the people, and even by the legislature, is commonly sought in the belief that this inner circle possesses information that cannot be made public for security reasons. That belief is, on the whole, mistaken—I speak on this point with some personal experience. The knowledge emanating from diplomatic, military, and secret service sources is regularly both extremely shortsighted and characteristically narrow. Often, it is directly misleading. As events continuously prove, this type of "intelligence" is plainly mistaken even about facts which should be within its limited reach.

But I have seen how it fascinates the inner circle, left in charge of policy decisions from day to day. Such a group is often made up of people with a mediocre intellectual ability which does not allow them to take the long, broad, and detached view of world developments; there is in the national democratic procedures nothing to prevent such a negative selection of policy-makers by election and appointment. As a conflict situation develops, they are, moreover, tempted to tamper with truth in their propaganda to their own people and to the world. Because honest people are not cynical liars, they soon end up by believing their own propaganda, which then tends to be still further divorced from any deep and objective understanding.

It is a common experience that such propaganda—this opportunistic twisting of the truth—is singularly ineffective abroad. At home, however, it is effective. It gains support from the emotions of naïve patriotism, to which I have already referred. At that point, the leaders of a nation's foreign policy, particularly in a democracy, become imprisoned by their own propaganda and its results to mislead the people as well as themselves. They will feel compelling reasons of internal policy to continue an aggressive foreign policy, even if they would otherwise be prepared to make a halt or consider a shift of line.

The social scientists in this situation, who have a deeper and broader knowledge of the facts, will be in a difficult position. Before the forces of public opinion thus created, they have to be bold indeed to stand up and criticize the foreign policy. And even if they should do it, they know that their influence cannot be either strong or immediate, for in the last instance it would amount to completely re-educating a people. The recognition of this—together with the fact that in some cases they themselves have been swayed by emotional patriotism that appeals to "closing the ranks"—will give most of them reasons for feeling that discretion is the better part of valor.

This all amounts to a restricting and redirecting impact of society on the pursuit of the social sciences, instead of the impact of social sciences upon society. For a scholar in the great liberal tradition, this would be a deeply discouraging trend, if it were to proceed unchallenged. As we all know, this is fortunately not the case. Realizing the extreme danger of the present drift in international relations, the academic community has stood up rather massively for calm critical reasoning, founded upon broad and deep knowledge, detachments and circumspections—even in foreign policy, it has taken its stand against the official, adventurous, shortsighted, automatic escalation. In this field, the escapist scientism that I have referred to has been given up. Our only hope—in the field of foreign policy as in that of national policies—is in democracy, but specifically in an enlightened democracy. Events press our profession to take the lead in making democracy enlightened by educating the people.

COMMENTARY

JULIA J. HENDERSON

It is not so often that administrators are allowed to comment publicly on the papers of eminent professors or that international civil servants are given the opportunity to contradict the "movers and shakers" of the international community—even after they have left our ranks. It is therefore, a particular pleasure to be invited to "discuss" Dr. Gunnar Myrdal's paper.

At the outset, I should like to say that it is obviously correct that we can do no more than to speculate about the impact of the social sciences on society. Furthermore, I agree generally with Professor Myrdal's comments concerning methodology in the social sciences on the assumption that he does not intend to slow down the search for quantification of social phenomena in areas where it is so far not very successful. I share his hope to see a new emphasis on institutional approaches and a more straightforward attempt to deal with values and qualitative factors. In my own field of political science, I was struck by a quotation from Robert Dahl's commentary on research into political behavior:

Yet it seems clear that unless the study of politics generates and is guided by broad, bold, even if highly vulnerable general theories, it is headed for the ultimate disaster of triviality.

Finally, I should like to suggest that empirical political science had better find a place for speculation. It is a grave though easy error for students of politics impressed by the achievement of the natural sciences to imitate all their methods save the most critical one: the use of the imagination.[1]

However, my main concern is to address myself to the central question raised by Professor Myrdal, i.e., "What difference does it make to policies and developments, if we can increase knowledge about society and liberate men's ideas from ignorance and irrational inhibitions?" On the whole, I have felt that Professor Myrdal has taken too pessimistic a view in his response to this question. When one considers how deep are the forces that move modern society, how encrusted with prejudice and emotion and how complex the process of decision-making in the modern world, the wonder is that social inventions, such as the Wicksell-Keynesian analysis cited by Dr. Myrdal; or his own work on *The American Dilemma*; or UNESCO's series on "Race and the Society" can have such profound impact on public policy within a generation.

[1] "The Behavioral Approach in Political Science," *American Political Science Review* (December, 1961), p. 772.

As an Administrator in the United Nations, whose role is to help make that bridge between social research and public policy, particularly as it applies to the development problems of those poverty-stricken nations of the Southern hemisphere, I have had many occasions to witness the speed with which ideas and social inventions (arising only in part from social research to be sure) sweep through the newly independent countries. In some of these instances, the speed of acceptance may even be due in some measure to the fact that social science has not produced evaluations of alternative measures for achieving the same objectives. I may take as an example the idea of "community development" which, I believe, may qualify as a social invention if not a social theory. Social scientists and particularly social workers in this country and in some others, had applied themselves, for a generation, to the theory and practice of "community organization," but until the 1950's there had been little systematic attention to the problems of developing the villages of the under-developed countries where 70–90% of the population lived. To be sure, hundreds of people of good will—missionaries, doctors, agriculturists representing religious societies and foundations or various utopian movements—had labored in villages in India, Syria, or Nigeria to induce change and to raise the standard of living, and some had even documented their experiences; but these efforts touched only a handful of villages and many of these efforts slowed down with the emergence of the strong movement for political independence after World War II. Largely through the voices of indigenous leaders representing their countries in the policy-making bodies of the United Nations and its specialized agencies, the idea that a vital partnership of national governments, village communities, and international technical aid could make a real difference in the living standards of masses of poverty-stricken people took hold in the United Nations by 1953. The idea had a social research base in one sense—the Preliminary Report on the World Social Situation, published in 1952, after reviewing the levels of health, education, employment and income around the world concluded that it was "the peasant in the stagnant village in the underdeveloped country who is the forgotten man of the twentieth century." It was in response to this call to action that Dr. Kummarappa, of India, declared that the United Nations must reach beyond national capitals, that it must lend a helping hand in mobilizing the vast human resources of the villagers, in raising their levels of aspirations, and providing them the knowledge and the tools necessary to undergird their own efforts. Four U.N. missions, over the period 1953–1956, visited Asia, the Caribbean, the Middle East and Africa, interviewing political leaders, administrators, extension agents, teachers, peoples' organizations, and even social scientists and out of their findings, the consultations of the international agencies concerned, and the deliberations of the Social Commission there emerged the principles and definitions of community development. In 1952, only India and Egypt had national policies and programmes labelled community development. By the end of the decade, every country in South-East Asia, from Afghanistan around the arc to the Philippines and Korea had adopted such programmes. Most of the Middle East States were experimenting with such programmes on a demonstration basis. African countries had already 5–10 years experience with programmes of mass education and community development in the English-speaking territories and cooperative development in the French-speaking, and after independence were attempting to adapt these programmes to new circumstances. The Latin American countries, struggling in the fifties with problems of political reform, were the last to take notice of this idea. Beginning about 1960, however, they have embraced this social invention with enthusiasm both as a political movement—witness "Acción Popular" in Chile, "Acción Comunal" in Colombia, "Cooperación Popular" in Peru— and as a two-way channel between the people and the economic planners.

As the movement has grown in importance, the attention of social scientists as well as social workers (in the broadest sense) to community development has been greatly intensified. Many such scientists have engaged in evaluation activities, others in preparing the studies which have provided the basis for widespread training programmes for professional and auxiliary community development workers. University institutes of Research cum Action in this field have sprung up in our own country as well as the developing countries themselves. It remains to be seen whether the scientific interest will remain when the politicians seek new panaceas and new labels to revitalize their development efforts. I can only express the hope that social scientists will not lose interest in the fundamental question, that is, the motivation of people to participate in the development of their communities (both local and national), and the most effective political and social organizational forms for achieving their development goals in the great variety of settings which the international community affords.

If, by this example, I have only supported Professor Myrdal's contention that social scientists have been followers rather than leaders, that they have talked to each other more than to the policy-makers, I would like to say that the social scientists are making a major contribution to the thinking going into the policy-making process in U.N. agencies, as well as in national governments in the area of urbanization. Since the mid-term censuses of the 1950's, demographers and sociologists have been bringing into clear focus the nature and scope of the urbanization process. Whereas most economists had long viewed urbanization as the natural and inevitable consequence of industrialization, the social science research of the fifties showed beyond doubt that it was a parallel and independent process and that the unhealthy consequence of this rapid growth was largely a product of the imbalance between the creation of jobs and the skill levels of the new labour supply. These facts, published not only in our demographic and social reports, but discussed with national and metropolitan administrators, economists, town planners, and social workers, in every region have led to higher priorities for industrialization, including problems of industrial location, housing and physical planning, and growing recognition that wider policies on population distribution are required in the interests of national development and levels of living.

If I may cite one final example of the impact of social science on social policy—and I do not, of course, claim to know the actual impact of these policies on *society* which is the broader topic to which Professor Myrdal has addressed himself—I would like to mention the work of an inter-disciplinary group of social scientists in preparing the 1961 *Report on the World Social Situation*, which was devoted to the theme "Planning for Balanced and Integrated Economic and Social Development." I choose this example for its relevance to some of Myrdal's comments on methodology in the social sciences. I agree completely with his contention that many of the efforts to borrow techniques from the natural sciences for application to economics and further to transfer them to other social sciences have produced unrealistic model-building. I would not be quite so sweeping in my criticism since it seems to me that some of the highly sophisticated mathematical work of a demographer like Jean Bourgeois-Pichat has produced demographic models which attracted the attention of the economic planners in a more effective way than many volumes of demographic analysis had done in the past. However, the point of my illustration is simply this—that a small team consisting of a social psychologist, two economists, a statistician and an anthropologist produced a profile analysis of social and economic indicators in 72 countries and defined the issues of inter-relationship of social and economic factors in development in such a way that, in the short space of five years, has had a highly significant impact not only on the work of the U.N. in the social field but on the structure of planning in more than a score of countries. For the very lack of research about which Professor Myrdal complains at the beginning of his paper, I cannot, of course, prove that the steadily growing number of countries which have established social departments within their planning organs would attribute that change to the work of the U.N. However, most Latin American countries would directly trace their interest in economic planning and the training of their planning personnel to the Economic Commission for Latin America (ECLA), and ECLA will certainly credit the 1961 World Social Report with its new interest in planning the social sectors of development. The Netherlands Government was directly influenced to the extent of contributing $1,000,000 for research in the inter-relationships of social and economic factors in development. The World Bank, as well as major foundations, has invested in particular social sectors such as planning for education. Here I would like to stop again to agree specifically with Myrdal's criticism of the superficiality of much of the work done by economists on "investment in man." I would hope he will take occasion to develop further his point that the "exercise has turned out to be not even a formulation of the real problems in education to be solved by the social scientists, if we want to take due consideration of education as an important development factor."

Since I appear to be more optimistic than Professor Myrdal about the impact of the social sciences on society, it will not surprise this audience if I am also more optimistic about the attractiveness of applied social sciences for a fair share of the most talented young people of our generation. I fully agree with him that an approach to the social sciences which concentrates on research techniques for their own sake, which avoids controversial issues, or focuses on studies of terminology is unlikely to attract our best young people. It is also obvious that the competition of the exact sciences is formidable, especially when the glamour of moon-shots may be added to the status of the young scientist. However, I would welcome either collaboration or opposing evidence from our academic colleagues of my own speculation that the period of social reform in which we are now engaged in this country may be attracting a highly motivated, talented group of young people into the social sciences. In any case, I am aware that deans of medical schools and even heads of physics departments in many American universities are lamenting the loss of talented graduate students to the social sciences and humanities.

In some other parts of the world in which I am interested, the social sciences in a modern sense hardly existed a decade ago, except as adjuncts of law and philosophy. The UNESCO Social Science Department, under the able leadership of Mr. Myrdal, made a significant contribution to the establishment of Social Science Departments in the universities of Latin America, Asia and Africa. In Latin America today, the attraction of the social sciences is supported by the natural inclination of the young to participate in the political and social reform of their countries. UNESCO's report on "The development of higher education in Africa" (1963) also shows the marked growth in the number of social science departments in the universities and a significant rise in the proportion of students undertaking their major work in these fields—it is difficult to believe that this attraction is only or primarily for the mediocre student, given the high interest in economic and social development in the new nations.

Finally, I would like to challenge Professor Myrdal's suggestion that the American social scientist is too timid to speak critically of his Government's foreign policy and is, indeed, too conscious of "grantsmanship" to permit himself to be objective in these areas heavily overlaid with emotionalism and patriotism. None of us would wish to deny that such people exist; but no one who has watched the course of the "teach-ins" and other forms of demonstrations against U.S. policy in South-East Asia, who has listened to the nation-wide seminar on U.S. policy toward China conducted on T.V. by our Senate Foreign Relations Committee, or who has listened to our President address the academic community at Princeton or in Chicago since last May could have any doubt that American social scientists have the courage of their convictions. I would join with Professor Myrdal in the underlying plea that the social scientist play his role more fully in introducing greater rationalization in the public mind in the making of foreign policy. In this connection, I should like to urge that all the social science disciplines should be more fully engaged in this effort. International affairs should not be considered the province of the political scientist, the international lawyer, or the student of diplomatic history any more than it should be the rightful study of sociologists, economists, and other social scientists. Indeed, the future of mankind may depend far more on our understanding of the development process in the great variety of cultures in the Southern hemisphere than it depends on knowledge of formal governmental forms of organization and existing power relationships.

COMMENTARY

EVELINE M. BURNS

The task of commenting on a paper by Gunnar Myrdal is no easy one. As always, what he has to say is stimulating and challenging because it is the product of his scholarship, his intuitive gifts, his profound concern for the human condition, and his engaging personal optimism. He also covers a vast amount of ground. Consequently, a commentator has to be selective and I can touch on only a few of his points. Furthermore, my own view of the role of the social scientist in contemporary society and my own social philosophy are so similar to his it will be difficult to avoid mere repetition of what he has said.

I stress his optimism, for although much of his paper is pessimistic in tone, he finishes, as always, on an optimistic note. He fears that we social scientists are lagging behind the physical scientists not only in the rate of our "scientific progress" but also in the impact we are having on society, and he proceeds to inquire why this should be so.

One can begin by asking whether it is indeed true that social science has been so backward and uninfluential. Perhaps, when we measure influence, we are unduly affected by our very high expectations of what we should have been able to achieve. The enormous influence exerted on their society by the late eighteenth and the nineteenth century social scientists—Adam Smith, Ricardo Malthus, Bentham and even J. S. Mill—may have given us an unduly high standard of the influence we should be able to exert. In any case, I would argue that even in our lifetime, the social scientists have been more influential than Myrdal seems to suggest. He himself admits the tremendous influence exerted by the ideas of J. M. Keynes and while, as he says, it took thirty years for these ideas to prevail, this is surely a very short time in the span of history for so major a revolution in thinking to occur. Professor Frankel, earlier in this symposium, reminded us of the great influence exerted by Marx and Freud. It is undoubtedly Myrdal's own modesty that prevents him from mentioning another influential social scientist, named Gunnar Myrdal, whose *American Dilemma* has had a profound impact on our thinking about the Negro problem, not merely because of its factual demonstration of the effects of segregation and discrimination on the Negro, but also because he showed that discrimination also creates a problem for whites—the dilemma brought about by the lack of correspondence between what white Americans were in fact doing and what their moral beliefs were, as expressed in what Myrdal has called the American Creed.

Social scientists are influencing our thinking in other ways, too. Our growing concern with the population problem is surely not unrelated to the work of a generation of demographers in making available to us a body of data whose implications we can no longer disregard. Our concern about poverty and income inequality owes much to the fact that over the last forty years the social statisticians have so greatly improved and enriched our fundamental knowledge and removed much of the alibi of ignorance of the facts.

Myrdal complains of the paucity of social inventions in the social science field. Here again, I think he is a little too pessimistic. The Cost of Living index is surely an "invention" that has not only given us an instrument to understand reality better, but it has also provided an essential tool in the development and application of social policies. Witness, for instance, the role of the Cost of Living index in wage negotiations and collective agreements or its use in contemporary social security programs as a measure by which to adjust benefits and payments.

The family budget is another social invention that has had an important impact on social policy, for it has served to give concreteness to vague ideas. Not only has it enabled men to envisage more clearly what it means to live at any given income level, but also it says to most people that, at the poverty level, one can afford to spend 22 cents a person per meal, and this means more than to tell them that the poverty standard for a family of four is $3,130 a year. By defining and structuring a concept, what the English economic historian Clapham once called "filling empty economic boxes," it has transformed a vague idea into an operational tool which can serve as the basis of policy where costs and gains, ways and means, can be evaluated. I would also argue that the concept of Gross National Product is a social science invention which has exerted a great influence on men's minds.

Myrdal would perhaps argue that these examples which I have cited are lowly inventions at best which are properly only instrumental in character; I do not agree. If we are interested in influencing social policy we need tools and operational concepts; furthermore, I do not believe it can be denied that their very creation influences the way people think about their society.

Even if we limit ourselves to inventions in the sense of the devising of new social institutions to achieve certain ends, I do not think the social scientists have been wholly barren. Social Insurance is surely one such invention. The Children's Allowance is another. So, too, is the idea of the Guaranteed Minimum Income in either of its two forms, the Negative Income Tax or the Universal Demogrant. In a broader sphere, I would claim the Grant-in-aid as an important social invention; internationally, such an institution as the International Monetary Fund is another.

I would thus prefer to rephrase Myrdal's question and ask, not why we are so far behind the natural sciences, but why we do not seem to be more influential than we are. Here Myrdal offers us some valuable clues. He suggests that the social sciences have perhaps not attracted their fair share of outstanding first-class people. I second his plea for more factual information in this area. But here again, I would suggest that such an inquiry might reveal that we are not doing too badly. If such social scientists as Myrdal himself, or Samuelson, Lazarsfeld, Parsons, or Merton, Titmuss or Galbraith had chosen to work in the physical rather than the social sciences can anyone doubt that today many of them would have been recipients of Nobel Prizes? We have some very brilliant people in our social science midst!

Myrdal deplores the present tendency of social scientists to depart from the honorable tradition of personal involvement in social action and the effort to bring about change—even to the extent of not trying to make their findings and theories understandable to the average man. As one who has always believed that the social scientist has an obligation to express his knowledge and ideas in terms that the ordinary person can understand as well as to become actively involved in movements for social change, I heartily agree with his castigation of those who escape into "scientism." It is indeed true that among economists, the Galbraiths, the Hansens, the Hellers, the Seymour Harris's, the Douglas Browns or the Friedmans—are all too few. Within the field of social welfare, too, we cannot deny that for a generation there has been a withdrawal into narrow professionalism and a growing tendency, as Myrdal puts it, "to address one another."

Yet even here, at the risk of being thought a Pollyanna, I must suggest that perhaps the picture is not quite as black as Myrdal paints it. With the growing role of government, more action-oriented social scientists have entered government employment than ever before *precisely* because they believe that it is here that they can most readily influence policy. The Council of Economic Advisers attracts a staff of professional economists who are strongly social-action oriented. The Social Security and Welfare Administrations are largely staffed at the professional level by social scientists and for the same reason. The Office of Economic Development in the

Department of Commerce, the Budget Bureau and even the Treasury abound with economists who exert an important influence on national policy and, as everyone knows, the Office of Economic Opportunity is swarming with socially active sociologists. Many, though by no means all, of these governmentally employed social scientists assume an anonymity and we may thereby be led to underestimate the degree of involvement of the social science profession in social action.

Furthermore, within the social welfare field, there are encouraging signs of change. The professional organizations are becoming more actively interested in social policy, even though they have yet to realize that those who claim to be heard because of their professional expertise must know whereof they speak, and social work education has until now produced pitifully few social workers who are knowledgeable in the policy area.

Indeed, it is here, I believe, that we come to the heart of our problem. More important than the possibility that social science may be failing to attract its fair share of the first-class minds, more significant than the withdrawal of social scientists from active participation in movements for social change, is the question of what it is we have to offer society. Myrdal suggests that we lag far behind the physical sciences in our ability to offer "undisputed truth in our findings." As he says, "In regard to all problems there are schools of thought with different gospels, among which the politicians and the citizens at large can choose according to their predilections." Myrdal attributes this to various factors; I would like to comment on two of them.

First of all, as he points out, the problems we deal with are indeed more difficult to solve. We have no constants as do the physical scientists. The data and variables with which we deal include the influence of human institutions and attitudes, and these change and interact and are difficult to measure. Consequently, even if we are able to demonstrate a causal relationship or a social science "law" it may be valid at a given time or for a society characterized by specified institutions and attitudes, but quite invalid at another time or in a different type of society.

I would add two other difficulties peculiar to the social sciences. We are inhibited from many types of experimental research because of our squeamishness about experimenting on human beings and our reluctance to penalize our control groups. And the rigorous testing of the accuracy of our predictions is made difficult by the very fact that we do, indeed, exert an influence. On the one hand, we may be led into an exaggerated estimate of their accuracy because of the effects of the self-fulfilling prophesy. On the other hand, a dire outcome we have predicted may not occur—not because we incorrectly interpreted the facts or drew wrong inferences from them, but because men do believe us and take steps to change the course of events.

This situation has important implications for the nature and methodology of social science research. Myrdal sharply criticizes what he calls "the strenuous and strained effort of contemporary social scientists to emulate the methods of the natural sciences." He is especially critical of their neglect of the influence of institutions and attitudes, and of the ways in which they try to rationalize this neglect. I share his view and only hope he is right in regarding it as a "temporary aberration into superficiality and irrelevance."

In our own field of social welfare this intoxication with the measurable and the "scientifically precise," as judged by the criteria applied to physical research, is very pronounced. Research, if it is to be respectable—and above all if it is to receive support from foundations or governmental grants—has come to be identified with adoption of the methods of investigation characteristic of the natural sciences which place strong emphasis on statistics and even mathematics. One consequence has been that the subjects of research are more and more determined not by the seriousness and urgency of social problems but by their amenability to study through the use of available research instruments and techniques or by the accidental availability of statistical or numerical data. Given the complexity of social phenomena, and the difficulty Myrdal has referred to of finding parameters and variables to represent human institutions and attitudes, it is not surprising that much of today's research takes the form either of working with highly simplified models which bear little relationship to the complexity of reality, or of an investigation of problem areas so limited that constants can be reasonably assumed and the techniques appropriately applied, but which are also so minute that the results are apt to be insignificant.

I would also question whether social welfare research is making the most effective use of what the social sciences have to offer. I detect a tendency for researchers to take some social science concept or "law" and test its generality by seeing to what degree it is valid or relevant in the social welfare field instead of formulating social welfare's own problems and then seeing how far any concepts or substantive knowledge from the social sciences might assist in their solution.

Perhaps part of the trouble is that we are too ambitious, or at least that we are in too much of a hurry. We want to formulate and test hypotheses and establish laws before all the necessary data are at hand and, even more importantly, before we have done the hard intellectual work of identifying all the more significant variables. For it is not enough to agree with Myrdal that social science research must take account of the role and influence of institutions and attitudes. What we lack is a theoretical base that would enable us to identify, as a first approximation to be tested by research, the *more relevant* attitudes and institutions. As I once said in discussing the institutional movement in economics on which Myrdal places his hopes, "The recognition of the interdependence of economic phenomena and institutions, and phenomena and institutions of all other kinds, is likely, unless we limit our fields, to result in a diffusion of energy and in an output of innumerable studies of the manifold aspects of human activity, which will be oriented by points of attack so diverse as seriously to hinder generalization or integration." [1]

These differences between the social and the physical sciences may even call into question the very concept of "science" as applied to the social sciences. Perhaps we may have to abandon what the economist Allyn A. Young once called the first article in the scientist's creed, namely, that "what appear to be arbitrary or capricious happenings can be fitted into a scheme which has no room for anything but dependable uniformity and regularity." We may have to agree with him that "no complete scientific synthesis of all the different social sciences is possible." [2]

[1] E.M. Burns, "Institutionalism and Orthodox Economics," *American Economic Review* (March, 1931), p. 85.

[2] Allyn A. Young, "Economics as a Field of Research," *Quarterly Journal of Economics* (November, 1927), pp. 1 and 5.

But this is a large topic and one with which I am not competent to deal. I want merely to suggest that even if the scientific status of the social sciences is uncertain or undefined, this does not excuse us for neglecting the more modest, but truly scientific task of discovering more about, and improving, our knowledge of reality. The accumulation of data about the nature and extent of a social problem or an analysis of how a specific social welfare program in fact operates, is regarded unfortunately as lowly and pedestrian work. Yet Myrdal reminds us—and it is his most optimistic point—that attitudes and institutions are not only all related to, and depend for their unaltered existence on, beliefs about reality, but also that these are often irrational. From this premise, it follows that knowledge which corrects these irrationalities will help to change attitudes and institutions. Examples of the influence of beliefs about reality on social attitudes (and thus on social policies) abound in the field of social welfare. The belief that unemployment was due primarily to unwillingness to work was indeed effectively destroyed not by social research but by the common experience of the great depression. But we still need studies of attitudes to work, in a society characterized by relatively high employment and incomes. Social science research is increasingly challenging the belief that the cause of poverty is to be sought primarily within the individual himself. But what are we doing to test the validity of the widespread belief that women have more children only in order to get more money from the AFDC program and look on it as a comfortable way of earning a living? For that matter, what steps have we taken to test the validity of our own belief that the AFDC requirement that the father be absent from the home has encouraged family break-up?

The second point in Myrdal's explanation of the greater difficulties of social research on which I would like to comment is his discussion of the role of social values. He tells us that there has never been, or never can be, a disinterested piece of social research. Valuations enter into our work from start to finish even if we manage to be unaware of it, and we must, he insists, state our valuations as clear and explicit premises of our research. But, he adds, the value premises should not be defined arbitrarily—they must be relevant and significant in the society under study.

I confess that this last admonition leaves me somewhat confused as to what he means by valuations. For surely in many cases, especially in social welfare research, the scientist who is also a social actionist may hold values that diverge sharply from those of his society. Indeed, his very purpose may be to change those prevailing social values. I can only conclude that Myrdal is using value premises in two senses: values as data and values as beliefs held by a researcher.

In the first sense, value premises as data, I take it he means that the social scientist must state his assumptions about the significant prevailing values and these must indeed be relevant and significant in the society he is studying. It is not realistic or scientific, for instance, to explain human behavior on the assumption that men are motivated solely by a desire for money or even material well-being. I take it that this is what Myrdal has in mind when he reproaches social science for disregarding the fact that human beings have souls. I cannot refrain from pointing out that when he is arguing that knowledge can change people's attitudes, the illustrations he gives lay great stress on the economic motive. Thus, he suggests that a knowledge of the *costs* of rural and urban slums to the rest of society may bring about a change of attitude toward measures for their elimination, and the Norwegian studies to which he refers seem to have been effective because they showed that "well-planned social welfare policies are profitable for all social classes."

But if Myrdal is indeed thinking of social values as data, the valuation problem does not seem to be a separate difficulty but rather a part of the larger problem of taking account of institutions and attitudes in any piece of social research.

In the second sense of value premises (namely, the values held by the researcher), it is indeed highly desirable that the scientist should state his own value premises as explicitly as possible if only to put the reader on his guard against possible biases. For it is true that what the researcher sees and embodies in his work will in some degree depend on what he is looking for, and to this extent there never can be any disinterested social research.

You may have observed that throughout my discussion I have been constantly thinking of the applicability of Myrdal's paper to the field of social welfare. It seems to me that what he is saying to us is that we should not be led into the trap of slavish imitation of the criteria and research methods of the physical sciences, that our methodology must invent some way of taking account of the influence of institutions, values and attitudes, that our research should focus on significant social problems and that even if our methodology is shaky we must do the best we can, that we should seize every occasion to influence our society by better documentation of reality, by expressing our findings and theories in terms that the ordinary citizen can understand and by not withdrawing from active participation in social change movements into a pure and sterile scientism. But remembering Myrdal's warnings about the influence of value premises, stated or unstated, on the findings of the scientist, I realize that it may indeed be true—in Myrdal's paper perhaps I have found only what I was looking for!

COMMENTARY

GEORGE F. ROHRLICH

I.

I find myself so thoroughly in agreement with Professor Myrdal, both in respect of his general position and as regards most of the specific points which he has made, that I feel my own best contribution might be to carry forward some of the themes he has broached. In doing so, my objective will be to examine more specifically the relevance of Dr. Myrdal's observations to some particular situations which are of concern to a great many of us here assembled.

I start—as, I venture to think, the great majority of us here do—from Dr. Myrdal's basic humanist position, sharing in his high hopes for the eventual reward of enlightenment, and endorsing his essentially utilitarian outlook upon the social sciences which sees so clearly that the most important test of their advance lies in their practical applicability for the common good. I share, likewise, Professor Myrdal's confidence of continued social progress. I am particularly encouraged by his prediction that in another 10 or 15 years some of today's tangential departures in the social sciences will have been recognized as such and will be taking a back-seat to a renewed interest in the institutional foundations of our social existence.

I fear, however, that neither the general progress referred to nor the reawakening among social scientists of a true and sustained interest in down-to-earth social problems, will come about by itself— or will come about if things are left to take their present course. To bring about such changes will, I think, take some doing. And it is to this task, as I see it, that I propose to devote my comments.

II.

The questions I would like to raise concern the necessary transformation of our society so that it is capable of producing those ingredients which Dr. Myrdal mentions as being present in his own country, Sweden, and which he views, at least by implication, as necessary prerequisites for planned social progress. In my understanding, these ingredients comprise the systematic study and pursuit of social policy, and the deliberate application of a social engineering approach to meet the social problems of the day as well as those of the foreseeable future. I am wondering, first, whether we in this country are offering suitable opportunities for training the men and women in the required attitudes and skills. Second, even if some of them manage to acquire the outlook and training called for, I wonder where they can apply them effectively—as things stand today—for the benefit of our society.

Let me explain my puzzlement. It strikes me that, unlike many countries of Europe, we have not (in the social science curricula of our colleges and universities) any component which could be called "social policy." Nor are we producing by any other means a corps of professionals to look at social policy in its broadest aspects.

We have trained and we are training economists, as we have trained and are training doctors and lawyers, in such a way as to make them competent to master certain tools of their respective trade. Little, if anything, is offered these students to cultivate social motivation in their work, or even to instill in them as much as a clear conception of the social problems to be solved within that particular sphere of our social existence on which their profession has—or purports to have or should have—significant impact. Where, for example, in the current American curricula for students of economics, do we find course offerings that deal with the socio-political agenda of the next 25 years? Or, to take the current medical school curricula, where do we find courses on problems of social medicine that would acquaint our future doctors with the social aspects of their chosen profession? And just how many of our law schools have course offerings designed to broaden the social perspective of our future generation of lawyers by offering courses on the philosophy of due process of law and the enforcement of basic rights in the administration of public welfare?

There is not anywhere in our big government a bureau that could rightfully claim as its concern the study and analysis of our social problem areas and the development of over-all social policy alternatives. Perhaps, then, we should not be surprised if in this great country of ours, with a long tradition of all kinds of social investigation and analysis, and with a government that commands the greatest research instrumentalities in the world, we find ourselves pursuing every now and then a hit-or-miss approach, "brainstorming" methods, a practice of simultaneous and frequently improvised departures in many directions all at once, as we become alerted to, and alarmed by, the existence of a social problem that has become acute. At the present time, the need for effective income maintenance is being widely and heatedly debated. Schemes to produce a guaranteed minimum income regardless of ability to work are being proposed with scarcely a reference to our existing social security system (and, incidentally, our manpower development efforts). It is as though this product of decades of planning and legislative effort—as there *has* been—had not proven itself worthy as a solid foundation upon which to build; or conversely, as if it had reached its culmination and were no longer susceptible to or in need of further development and improvement.

Our schools of social work are about the only places in this country today where there *is* being cultivated an intense concern with certain aspects of the problem complex of social progress. Social welfare, obviously, is of paramount interest to those schools and to their student bodies; social welfare policy is an established part of *their* curricula. But, unless I am misled by my very incomplete knowledge, I sense another limitation there.

Let me pose this problem—or, at any rate, cite the situation that impresses me as such—by recalling to you another telling point made by Professor Myrdal: "Our discoveries and inventions in the

social field," he has stated, "must generally be applied by collectives."
To this I would like to add that, conversely, and no less important,
our social discoveries and inventions must generally be applied *to*
collectives as well. Yet, it sometimes seems as though many of those
immersed in the study or practice of social welfare were incapable
of extricating themselves from their warm and humanitarian concern for the specific problems (of an individual, a family, or small
group) long enough to view the larger matrix—to discover the
generic roots of comprehensive problem complexes. While they
have, in such rich measure, the motivation which economists and
sociologists nowadays often lack, they seem to have greater difficulty
—in contrast to earlier generations of social reformers—in looking
beyond individual social welfare services to social welfare in the
aggregate, and in broadening their vista to encompass not just
social welfare policy but also social policy in the broad sense.

Perhaps I am generalizing too loosely. Yet, if there *is* substance
to my supposition, this combination of a peculiar want of motivation amongst the prevailing types of social scientists of our day and
time on the one hand, and the widespread lag in broad social perspective among students and protagonists of social welfare on the
other hand, may go far toward explaining the paradox referred to
by Professor Myrdal: neither group has had a very significant impact
either in arousing public interest or in steering public policy as far
as the current wave of anti-poverty and anti-discrimination efforts
is concerned.

III.

To be sure, there have been (at various turning points of our
interwar and postwar history) certain legislative and other significant
events that revealed a clear and comprehensive long-range perception
of national problems and objectives. The Social Security Act of
1935, the Employment Act of 1946, and the Presidential Commission on National Goals of 1960 stand out as such, probably also the
Manpower Development and Training Act of 1962 and the several
Education Acts.

Perhaps another (and possibly even more important) turning
point may come about as a consequence of the Report of the

National Commission on Technology, Automation and Economic Progress published earlier this year. That report speaks of the need for a "system of social accounts" to help us put into perspective the full impact upon our social fabric of our gainful pursuits and of our public policies (or lack thereof), and raises the prospect of a "future-oriented" society conscious of the "need to set national goals." [1]

If this report, and certain other current straws in the wind, may be taken as true indications of a new national course, then the development of social statesmanship—its institutionalization, and the question as to where the recruits for it will come from—are problems which pose themselves with particular urgency.

It is at precisely this point that the issue is joined. The full impact of the title of this symposium, of Professor Myrdal's paper and, indeed (if I may be so bold as to remind ourselves of it) the very name of the School whose 50th Anniversary we are celebrating here today—the *application* of the social sciences, to wit: their societal impact—comes to the fore as a challenge for our time. Stated in terms most immediately relevant to many of us here assembled, the challenge is this: Will this school—and other schools like it which are offering instruction and training within the wide domain of the social sciences—succeed in turning out graduates who are qualified, competent, eager and ready to apply a broad-gauged social science knowledge (in some part of which they have acquired a specialization in depth) to solving the problems of our society? The answer may depend on our ability to instill in our students two important things: social motivation and concern, and scientific-technical competence relevant thereto. Either attainment alone and by itself is too little.

What this means in today's social science curricula is that wherever an aloofness from the economic, social, or political realities threatens either to remove students from the social scene or to blunt their social concern and to encourage social escapism, appropriate confrontations ought to be built into revised curricula as part of the required training. Where, in today's social work curricula,

---

[1] *Technology and the American Economy*, Report of the National Commission on Technology, Automation and Economic Progress, I (February, 1966), pp. 95, 105, and 106.

the emphasis is altogether or preponderantly on preparing students for person-to-person or person-to-group relationships, there needs to be added a "macro-social" dimension. (I am using this term in a somewhat loose analogy to the commonly accepted term "macro-economics.")

In summary, I do think we need to cultivate the ability to view society as a whole, to think in terms of social aggregates and corresponding social policy approaches, and to discern the interdependence of social problem complexes among themselves, and with the public interest. This is to call for the fostering of social architects and social strategists—alongside the conventional and much needed social practitioners; and, in a general way, to imbue professional people of all kinds with a developed social conscience and perception.

Beyond this—and here we look to developments which are only indirectly subject to being influenced by many of us here—we shall have to make a place in our society and government for this new type of graduate and professional. We have to be working toward a national commitment to social goals, and an institutionalized national concern with long-term policies conducive to their attainment.

The difference between going on—despite the best of intentions —producing successive improvisations, mostly palliatives conceived *ad hoc* and of limited impact, or hopefully—and in line with Professor Myrdal's prognosis—bringing the best of our social science insights to bear upon the real problems of our society, may be the orderly and peaceful evolution of our society, and of global society, for the betterment of the human condition.

THE RESPONSE

GUNNAR MYRDAL

We are at the end of the conference and I feel that I should be brief in my response to the discussants. This is the easier since, as they have been selected, we broadly share the same views.

I may sound a little more pessimistic than they. But I believe this is mostly due to the personal accident of life that I happened to start out as a more naïve believer in the golden political optimism of Enlightenment than anybody I know, except my wife. Then, early, I became responsible for housing reform in Sweden and learned the hard way that houses live as long as human beings and represent a considerable investment. The housing problem cannot be solved by a simple rationalization of our thoughts and the enactment of a legislative act, but requires carefully planned and costly endeavors over decades. Soon after, I came to work on race relations in America. There, even more, any improvement must be the result of political action on a broad front, stretching over generations; a final and complete solution remains a vision which might never come true. Next, I worked as a U.N. official for ten years and found how difficult it is to get governments to agree even on the most sensible proposals in their common interests. Now, finally, I am working on the development problems of the dismally poor peoples in South Asia; development there is another dream which might never come true. Towards the end of a long life devoted to social science and social reform, I find it more difficult to feel happy about my own achievements than those of my colleagues who started out with lower pretensions for the practical importance of faith and reason.

Coming over to more tangible matters, I listened with great interest to Julia Henderson's attempt to defend a greater role for simplified mechanical models in the study of the development problems of underdeveloped countries. The important point is, however, that for examples she chose the demographic models. But they belong to a natural science: the relationships between the biological events of births, deaths and age distribution form a definite and simple mechanism. But when we want to take into consideration the causes of changes in births and deaths, we are out in the wide field of attitudes and institutions, and our model-thinking has reached the limit of its usefulness.

I want to underline one thing that Julia Henderson pointed out, namely the importance of the work of the international secretariats. It is they who have given us the basis of factual information—about income levels, international trade and finance, demographic changes, etc.—upon which the whole discussion of the development problems of underdeveloped countries is founded. Compared with these fundamental research achievements, what we have done in the ivory towers of academic research is rather secondhand.

I agree with George Rohrlich that we should now be educating social engineers. I wish your school would take its name—School of Applied Social Sciences—seriously and begin to do something about it. The United States with its big urban and rural slums will certainly need—for a long time—social workers of the conventional type more than those Western countries who are socially more advanced than the United States. Nevertheless, America now needs more people trained to assist in the planning of social reforms, and—when they are once legislated—in the carrying out of these reforms. And I believe that it is also important to widen the mental horizon of the everyday social worker so that he can see his activity in this broader perspective of reforming society. I agree also with my old friend Eveline Burns that we should train economists to take a forward look over the next twenty-five years and to delineate the policy alternatives open to us.

It is rather astonishing how the social scientists succeed to avoid taking up the really important problems. To take two examples from the study of the Negro problem in America, we can first note that one of the damaging stereotyped beliefs which is commonly held not only by uneducated but also educated people in America is that Negroes have a peculiar smell. The liberal American used to add that we whites also have a smell of our own which is repugnant to the Chinese. Twenty-five years ago there was only one professor who had cared to make the obvious empirical experiment of taking sweat from white and Negro athletes in test tubes and have his students try to say what came from Negroes and what from whites; the result was, of course, a random distribution. A second, even more damaging stereotype, is the "black-baby myth," which perpetrates the superstition that a drop of Negro blood in either one of the parents can produce a black baby. Until Louis Wirth and I made a careful study, showing that children of mixed marriages *always* had a color between their parents, nobody had thought it worthwhile to study the reality that should correspond to the myth.

Similarly now, the several thousands of university economists—

with too few exceptions—have devoted themselves to other-worldly studies. When the public awareness of the pathological poverty in America's urban and rural slums rose to an intellectual and moral catharsis, this was the result of the observations and publications of journalists, social workers and politicians, not economists. We cannot be very proud of our profession's contribution to social change in America.